Ministry of Culture Publications of the Republic of Turkey/1725

Dîvân-i Kebîr

Meter I
Bahr-i Recez

Mevlânâ Celâleddîn Rumi

translated by
Nevit Oguz Ergin

Current Walla Walla

Dîvân-i Kebîr

Copyright © 1995 by
Nevit Oguz Ergin
&
Turkish Republic Ministry of Culture

ISBN 975-17-1506-7

First Printing 1995
Printed in the United States of America
in a joint publication by

Turkish Republic
Ministry of Culture

&

Current
P.O. Box 247
Walla Walla
WA 99362

Dîvân-i Kebîr

Mevlânâ Celâleddîn Rumi

Introduction

At the suggestion of the government of Turkey, 1995 has been announced to the world by the United Nations as the *Year of Tolerance*.

In the last years of our century, our world is witnessing an increase in nationalism, fanaticism in religions, and racial intolerance. The concept of tolerance with its ideas and possibilities appears as a way to fight these unfortunate situations.

What is tolerance? Tolerance can be explained as having a fair and objective attitude toward those whose opinions and behaviors differ from our own and showing respect for and interest in the ideas and practices of others.

The boundaries of tolerance can be drawn by not harming basic human rights in any way, either directly or indirectly.

The concept of tolerance will be addressed frequently during this year. Thoughts and views will be propagated. Benefits will be derived by utilizing the constructive, unifying, educational characteristics of this notion.

When 1995 became the Year of Tolerance, it added new excitement and dimensions to our ability to offer our literary and cultural heritage to our people and to the rest of the world.

When tolerance is mentioned, certainly the name of Mevlânâ Celâleddîn, a great thinker and poet who has a matchless place in Turkish-Islamic literature and culture, comes to the minds of all intellectuals.

Mevlânâ's thoughts are so profound that their depth cannot be reached. Their horizon constantly expands. Their exuberance never ceases, never scares us, but rather always caresses, provoking thought and unraveling tangled feelings. His thoughts have found many followers here and around the world and attracts them to his philosophy.

One of Mevlânâ's greatest works is *Dîvân-i Kebîr*. It was prepared in seven volumes by Abdülbâki Gölpinarli, based on the two most dependable volumes of the *Dîvân-i Kebîr* of the Mevlânâ Museum in Konya, and was published by our Ministry in 1992. This time, the *Dîvân-i Kebîr* is being translated into English and co-published in the U.S.A. by our Ministry. We are involved in this great project because it is the Year of Tolerance.

I will leave everyone with our Mevlânâ's lines alone. I wish happy days in a more tolerant, peaceful world.

Ercan Karakaş
Minister of Culture
Ankara, Turkey
1995

Translator's Note

This is a humble attempt of an English translation of the late distinguished Turkish Scholar Abdülbâki Gölpinarli's (d.1982) seven volumes of the *Dîvân-i Kebîr* of Mevlânâ Celâleddîn.

According to Gölpinarli, his translation of the *Dîvân* was based on the following sources:

    1.   Two volumes of the *Dîvân* which were compiled between July 2, 1367 and October 13, 1368 by Hasan ibni Osman-al Mavlavi. This *Dîvân* has 290 pages, and the volume dimensions are 0.325 x 0.47 meters. It is registered at the Mevlânâ Museum in Konya as No. 68 and No. 69.

    2.   The *Dîvân* registered at the Library of the University of Istanbul, No. 334, which was compiled in the 15th century.

    3.   The *Dîvân* owned by Gölpinarli, prepared in 1691 in Baghdad. Later, this *Dîvân* was donated to the Mevlânâ Museum in Konya.

    4.   Eight volumes of *Kulliyat-i Shems ya Divan Kebir* prepared by Bedî-uz-Zaman Furûzan-fer, prepared in 1965 (1345 S.H.).

There are many other versions of the *Dîvân-i Kebîr*, but these are the most dependable ones.

Mevlânâ did not write, but rather recited the poems. Most of them were recorded by assigned people called Secretaries of Secret (Katibal esrar) .

The *Dîvân*'s language is 13th century colloquial Farsi. However, there are numerous *gazels*, or poems, written in Arabic and Greek. In addition, there are Turkish words and phrases spread throughout the *Dîvân*'s pages.

There are 21 meters in the *Dîvân*. The first volume has 12,493 verses; the second has 4,052; the third has 4,526; the fourth has 4,180; the fifth has 6,684; the sixth has 4,002; and the seventh has 8,892. All together, the *Dîvân* has 44,829 verses.

We are starting with the first meter, *Bahr-i Recez*. In the original *Dîvân-i Kebîr*, the meters were compiled according to their ending rhyme scheme and the last alphabet letter of their rhyme, not in chronological order. This first meter has the rhyme scheme *Müstef'ilün Müstef'ilün Müstef'ilün Müstef'ilün*.

I am grateful to the Ministry of Culture of Turkey and, in particular, the Minister of Culture Ercan Karakaş, for their support and encouragement which have enabled me to bring the first meter of this gigantic work to reality.

I am also indebted to Mrs. Terry Peart for the years she has spent not only reading my handwriting, but understanding, typing and editing it.

I would like to thank our Editor, Ms. Millicent Alexander, our Art Director, Ms. Susan Archibald, our Publisher, Mr. David Hiatt of *Current*, and Ms. Laura Sjöberg, Mr. Ali Mahabady and Dr. Erdogin Erol, as well as the many others, too numerous to name here, for their help and encouragement.

It is with great excitement and humility that I bring this treasure, in its entirety for the first time, to the English-speaking world.

Nevit Oguz Ergin
Translator

Leather binding of *Dîvân-i Kebîr* (c.1368)
registered at the Mevlânâ Museum in Konya.

Left-hand page of the Table of Contents of *Dîvân-i Kebîr* (c.1368) registered at the Mevlânâ Museum in Konya, Turkey.

Right-hand page of the Table of Contents of
Dîvân-i Kebîr (c.1368) registered at the Mevlânâ
Museum in Konya, Turkey.

Bahr-i Recez

Müstef'ilün Müstef'ilün Müstef'ilün Müstef'ilün

First page, Gazel 1, Verse 1 (shown opposite in
English) of *Bahr-i Recez, Dîvân-i Kebîr* (c.1368),
registered at the Mevlânâ Museum in Konya, Turkey.
Müstef'ilün Müstef'ilün Müstef'ilün Müstef'ilün
represents the rhyme scheme of the meter.

1.

O Beloved, whose Love gives arms and wings
To the flyers in the sky of happiness
And makes them go higher and higher,
Different ecstasies come to the spiritual person
Through Your chains of Love.

"I don't like anything to set." [1]
Those words are devoid of appearances.
Forms and shapes from You
Are seen every moment
By those eyes that see hidden things.

Hearts are upside down because of You.
The earth has turned into a sea of blood.
I cannot call You "Moon," O Beloved,
Who has been above the moon, above time.

The mountain is split open with Your grief,
And that grief falls down to the bottom
To blaze with glittering flames.
All these favors, all these beauties
Have grown and developed
Because they acquired a drop of blood
From Your favor and Grace.

O the support and confidence of all great men,
Consider us among them.
As You know, tails will follow heads.

You have created such a great man out of dust [2]
That all the angels are jealous.
The Soul is penniless compared to Your wealth.
All goods and fortune fall to the ground underfoot.

A person reaches the height of the sky
If You become his arms and wings.
That person carries the sign of beauty on his face
And becomes more and more beautiful.

Assume I'm a thorn, a bad one.
But the thorn and rose go together.
When a jeweler weighs gold,
He puts barley as a weight
On the other side of the scale.

Actions go with ideas;
Goods come from the earth.
This situation appears in words;
The words are the sign of situations.

The beginning of the universe
Is confusion, tumult.[3]
The end is a shake and a quake.
Love and gratitude are the same as complaints.
Peace and comfort go hand-in-hand
With jolts and shakes.

Dawn is the decree of the sun.
Love of God, the Sultan's monogram,
And "the time of Union has come now:"
Love is interpreted this way.

Look at the One
Who is the compassion of the universe.[4]
Look at how He uplifts, gives status to the poor.
Mantles are as bright as the moon.
Shawls smell like roses.

Love is the whole thing.
We are only pieces.
Love is the sea of no end.
We are a drop of it.
He brings forth hundreds of proofs.
We can find our way only through them.

The sky turns only with Love.
Without Love, even the stars
Are eclipsed, extinguished.
With Love, hunched back *dal*[5] become *elif*.[6]
Once *elif* loses Love, it turns into *dal*.

The word is the Fountain of Life,
Because it originates
From the Love of the knowledge
Of the real truth of things.
Don't keep Love away from your Soul,
So that your good deeds may bear fruit
And keep growing.

The word is enough, even if it is scarce,
For the one who understands its meaning,
But it is never enough for the one
Who sees only appearances.
To him, the words are weak and pale.

It doesn't matter
If too many poems have been said.
Wouldn't it be better
If the sea were full of pearls?
The camel can keep going stage by stage
With the pleasure derived from poems.

2.

That hodja's[7] feet got stuck in the mud
In our neighborhood.
Let me tell you his story.
Do you remember the proverb,
"The eye becomes blind when fate comes?"

He used to boast cruelly,
Tuck up his trousers
So they wouldn't touch the ground.
He used to walk pompously.
He made fun of Lovers
And used to accept Love as a plaything or toy.

There are so many birds unaware of the trap,
Flying without knowing that an arrow of trouble
Is coming from the hand of fate.

That man was also dead drunk,
Passed out of himself,
Clapping his hands, making fun of Lovers,
And, with the illusion of his greatness,
He attempted to wrestle with God.

He wasn't aware of what was coming to him.
He used to raise his head to the sky.
Gold and silver were in his pockets.
Bravo, bravo sounded in his ears.

He was exalted by the people's applause,
By those who knelt down in front of him,
By those poets who praised him
And gave foolish talks.

Nobility has its own disaster,
Because kindness appears as greatness in man.
The ones who fawn create illusion
And make the person ill.

Hodja gave money thinking he was doing favors.
Actually, he didn't create that money.
How could someone be generous
With someone else's money?

He turned into a pharaoh and a Sheddad.[8]
He became a sack filled with air.
He was an ant, then changed into a snake,
And finally into a dragon.

Love is like the staff of Moses.
With the Divine secret,
Love threw an arrow from ambush.
Our hodja was bent like a bow
From the wound of that arrow.

He fell suddenly to the ground
Like a man with a seizure,
Started growling and convulsing.

He lost everything,
Became naked and disreputable.
Even his enemies felt sorry for him.
His relatives cried
As if there were a death in the family.

He was turned into a pharaoh like Nemrud.[9]
Really, he kept saying, "I am God."
When his neck was broken,
He realized his state
And started crying and calling out,
"O our God, O our God."

His face became pale like saffron.
He had no wound but the one opened
By the eyes of a beautiful face with sugar lips.

Shall we be more amazed
By the arrow of that beauty or by her bow?
Are her eyes more beautiful than her lips?
Is she more disloyal than the world?
Is she more concealed, or is the phoenix?

Let me tell you the secret of how to test Lovers.
Come back to your senses, free yourself
From this secret lock and chain.
Open your ears. Listen.

But how can a person open his ears
If he's out of himself
And doesn't know where his ears are?
"God does whatever He desires"[10]
Is the only rule that restores the mind.

Hodja's wings were broken like a mosquito's.
He yelled and screamed in torment
And started to cry from Ayse's[11] love-telling.
"A curtain has been drawn over my eyes,"
Said the hodja.

"Since you've gone, we've been ruined.
We're separated from you.
Alas, alas! Without you,
Life is death.
Please come back to us of your own will."

"My mind has been pawned to you.
Is there anyone to help me in my grief?
My Heart is subject to your trials.
It has fallen in the middle of death's hell
And keeps burning."

O yelling, crying hodja,
Your hands and feet were safe before
Whenever fate and accident hit them.
But you broke so many Hearts
Before this moment
That now their punishment has found your feet.

Be thankful to God that your punishment
Came from the side of Love.
But leave temporary Love,
Because real Love is God's Love.

The experienced veteran puts a wooden sword
In the hand of his son
Simply as a tool for training.

To Love another human
Is like that wooden sword.
When it ends in disaster,
Love turns toward a merciful God.

At first, Joseph, son of Jacob,
Was in love with Zeliha.
This lasted for years.
In the end, he experienced God's Love,
And it was then
That Zeliha fell in love with Joseph.

At first, she stayed away from Joseph,
Who had tried to touch her shirt.
In the end, Zeliha tried to tear Joseph's shirt.

"That's my retaliation," she said, "I got even."
Joseph said, "God's Love makes this
Such a funny kind of thing."

The one who desires becomes the desired one.
The one at the bottom rises to the top.
With His blessing, He makes many people
The Kible[12] to their prayer.

Here, words become thinner.
Breath doesn't fit in the mouth.
Now I want to use tongue-twisting words,
Because it's the right place.

He said, "Who am I?
I'm a figure made out of dust."
The one who casts Remil[13]
Draws, right or wrong, many lines on the ground.

Tell these words to our hodja, then listen.
Hodja said,
"Love set fire to my beard and burnt me.
Why have you left me?"

"O noble hodja, I left, but I came back quickly
To tell your situation to the people."

What could a silly man possibly tell?
How could a particle from the sun
Or a drop from the ocean
Explain this endless adventure?

When He shows you a small piece,
You'll understand the rest,
Just as you do when merchants show you
A handful of wheat from the barn
For buying and selling the grain in the silo.

When you see the sample,
You'll know the rest;
You'll know what kind of flour you'll get.

You're also like an old barn.
Dip in your hand
And pick up a handful of wheat from the pile.
See what kind of wheat you are,
Then take it to the mill.

That world looks like a mill.
This one is like a threshing floor.
Whatever you are here, bran or wheat,
That's what you are there.

Go on. Leave this obstinacy, O obstinate one.
Look. That hodja is waiting.
The one who has done his work halfway
Is rushing.
He says, "Come on now."

"O hodja, tell us, how are you?
Why did you stay in this land of troubles?
You're tired and afflicted with incurable pains,
Covered with blood and dirt."

The hodja answered, "Help, O Moslems.
Watch your Hearts. I've been wounded.
Be careful that something like this
Doesn't happen to you.

"I used to blame lovers
When I saw them suffering.
I laughed at them with a Heart full of malice
And called them names, using bad words."

"Woe to the one
Who slanders and ridicules people.
The one who says bad things,
He will get back exactly what he says."[14]

Is this the mouth of a human
Or the hole of a snake, a scorpion?
Close this hole with mud and straw.
Don't let friends be bitten.

Fall in Love. Forget names and titles.
Leave the grains, leave the trap.
Name the stone 'gold.'
Name sugar 'grief and suffering.'

3.

O parrot who has Jesus' breath,[15]
O sweet-voiced Beauty, nightingale,
Come with the melodies,
Adding Soul to Soul.
Make Venus confused and lost in space.

Claim your Beauty.
Let hundreds of enemies,
Hundreds of friends, known and unknown,
With yellow saffron faces and wet eyes
Become the witnesses.

Grief makes everyone cry.
Men, women, all wail
Because of grief.
Save us from grief,
Because it's become like a dragon of cruelty.

O beautifully-voiced Sweetheart,
Poke the belly of grief
With Your hard, soft melodies.
With Your justice, a tumult will be dropped
In the land of Absence.

Remember, our Cupbearer fills
Hundreds of water bottles with air,
Turns Souls into Ferhad[16]
For the Love of sweet-faced Shirin.

Your Heart, like an Archangel,
Gives life to man, who is made of mud.
Please blow the breath of God in our ear.

We've fallen to the ground
Like a heap of winnowed grain.
Grain and straw are mixed in us.
Give us a breeze from the wind of Soul.
Separate the grain from the straw.

Do us a favor. Let grief go to grief,
Joy to the joyful,
The rose to the rose garden.
Soul will rise to the sky.

Those beautiful grains' ears
Listen for God's compassion.
Their hope is in the morning breeze.
That's why they remain in the prison of earth.

Do a favor. Soul's work shines like gold,
Embraces the Beauties.
Soul's feet will become its head;
Straws will turn into amber.

Be silent! In one breath, if permitted,
I would tell the secret
That no one dares utter in the ear of his brother.

4.

O restless wind of ours
Which doesn't stop anywhere,
Say this to the rose for us:
"O rose, the one who escaped
From the rose garden
To be made into rose petal preserve
By mixing with sugar!

"O rose, you were sugar originally,
You deserve the sugar."
Sugar is good.
To be a rose is also good,
But to be loyal is better than both.

Touch your cheek to the cheek of sugar.
Get the taste of it. Give perfume to it.
Try to alleviate the pain of separation
With the help of sugar.

Once you become the conserve of roses,
You are food for the Soul,
Light for the eyes.
Pull your Heart away from the rose.
It's different now.

You were living with thorns
Just like the mind
Who is the friend of Soul.
Ascend from earth to the sky stage by stage
Until you meet Him.

When you walk among the people,
You walk on a secret path
From garden to garden.
You go to the Source
Where all these forms and shapes appear.

O rose, you are a rare bird,
Flying the opposite way of others
Because your news comes
From that other direction.
Leave your arms and wings.
Come without head or feet.

O rose, you've seen all.
That's why you're smiling at the world.
That's why you're tearing your clothes.
O red-kaftaned trickster!
O strong, healthy brave!

The roses are raining
From the sky to the rose garden, shouting,
"Anyone who wants stairs to the sky
Should throw his Soul to grief."

Come to your senses.
Try to get out of the bottle of the Master
Who makes rosewater like sweat.
Become like a Soul out of its container.

We were like you once.
Now we've become Soul.
Come. You must become Soul, too.
You'll have good luck, good fortune,
And a very rosy face.

When I say 'conserve of roses,'
I mean the Grace of God and our existence.
You see, our existence is like iron;
God's Grace is the magnet.

14

The mind is like a mirror.
The mirror maker
Causes torture with His flames
Because He doesn't want us.
He says, "I want you without you."

O the One who says words smells like musk!
Come back to yourself.
There is no end to these talks.
I won't tell anyone
The things You've told me.

O Shems of Tebriz,
Tell the secret of the Sultans
Without sound, without color, without smell.
If there is no sun,
There will be no light of dawn.

5.

O Sultan of our body and Soul!
O One who makes us smile and show our teeth!
O One who puts salve
On our body's and Soul's eyes!

O my Beautiful, the moon is embarrassed
Seeing Your light, Your height.
Our blood should be sacrificed to You.
When Heart sees You, it says,
"Divine fate has come. Divine fate has come."

We become a ball for You,
Fitting the curved end of Your club.
Sometimes You call us into places of fun.
Sometimes You push us into places of trouble.

Sometimes You put us to sleep.
Sometimes You send us to reason.
Sometimes You throw us
To the world of existence,
Sometimes to the desert of Absence.

He gives thanks to the Master.
Sometimes he yells and screams, "Alas!"
Sometimes he goes to serve Leylâ.[17]
Other times he becomes God's drunk,
God's crazy one.

You torment the Soul,
Make him crazy, insane.
Sometimes You make him enjoy solitude.
Sometimes You make him fond
Of ostentation and hypocrisy.

Sometimes he wants gold,
Then other times spreads earth on his head.
Sometimes he thinks he's Caesar.
Sometimes he wears
Old, patched and worn-out mantles.

What a strange tree he is.
Sometimes an apple is grown,
Sometimes a pumpkin.
At one time he yields poison,
At another, sugar.
He causes trouble sometimes,
And other times he is the remedy.

What a strange river he is.
Sometimes he becomes water, sometimes blood.
He turns into ruby-colored wine or milk,
Or sometimes health-giving honey.

Sometimes he weaves knowledge in the Heart.
Sometimes he destroys one's knowledge.
Sometimes he achieves superiority,
Other times he sees
Every trouble and misfortune.

One day he becomes Master Muhammed.
One day he turns into a tiger, then a dog.
Sometimes he becomes a mean enemy.
Other times he becomes a father, mother or kin.

Sometimes he becomes a thorn, then a rose.
Sometimes he is the vinegar,
Other times the wine.
Sometimes he plays the drum.
Sometimes he becomes a drum
And is hit by a mallet.

Sometimes he falls in love
With his five senses and six dimensions.
Sometimes he wants good spirits.
But sometimes, like a lost camel in the desert,
He wanders around.

Sometimes his aims and hopes
Are as deep as a well-digger's.
Sometimes he is among the treasures
Of a Karun[18] who hides his treasures.
Sometimes he is like Jesus
And ascends to the sky.

In the end, when Your grace opens his way,
Our Sheyyad[19] sings one tune
And is saved from changing from color to color.
He becomes crazy and dips into one color
Like an early morning sun.

He dives into the sea like a fish.
His garden, his meadow, his country become sea.
His coffin, his grave and everything else
Are dead, a plague to him, except that sea.

When he slips out of those colors,
He slips into the jar of Jesus.
God's color appears to do God's wishes.

He is saved from malice, from modesty.
He is saved from running and stopping
Like the millstone turning around the pin.
He is saved from 'come and go.'

"We open your door, really,
So you can keep your friend next to you.
We merge your coming generation with you.
This is the reward of Love. [20]

"We tie your waist tightly.
Really, we forgive your sins.
You gave thanks to God. That's the reason.
Thanks brings contentment."

Müstef'ilün, Müstef'ilün, Müstef'ilün, Müstef'ilün.[21]
The door of explanation is closed.
It is better for us to be silent.

6.

O Cupbearer, O Cupbearer,
Today You and I exist here
And have fallen into deep water.
Let's find out who knows how to swim.

If a flood covers the earth
With waves as big as camels,
The birds don't have to worry.
They think of nothing
While flying in the sky.

Our face shines with gratitude.
We are mixed like fish into the waves of the sea.
Sea and flood give life to fish
And make them more lively.

O Master, give us a boat.
O water, rise, engulf us with your waves.
O Moses, Son of Imran,
Hit the sea with your staff.[22]

This wine causes a different kind of drunkenness
In every head,
But the Love of that Cupbearer
Is enough for me.
You can have the rest of it.

The Cupbearer grabbed
All the drunks' hats yesterday.
Today He's serving cup after cup of wine
To take our mantles away.

O Beautiful One, of whom
The moon and Jupiter are jealous,
You are with me secretly, like a fairy,
Pulling me nicely, but not telling me
Where You're leading me.

O both of my eyes, light of my eyes,
Wherever I go, You are with me.
If You want, pull me toward the tavern,
Make me drunk,
Or pull me toward Nothingness.
Annihilate me!

Accept this world as Mount Sinai.
We also want manifestation like Moses.
Every moment God manifests,
And every moment
The mountain is broken into pieces.

A time comes when it becomes green,
Another time, extremely white,
Clear and beautiful.
One time it becomes pearl,
Then later, red amber.

O the ones who want to reach Him, see Him,
Look in the mountain places where He manifests.
O mountain, what kind of wine did you drink?
We've become drunk. Come, O friend, come.

O Owner of the garden, Gardener,
Why do You hold us?
Why don't You let us be free?
If we eat the grape, You take our turban.

7.

O Beloved whose light
Comes from behind the curtains,
Your light and warmth
Are like summer for us.
Take us to the rose garden.
Our Hearts are fiery like summer.

O salve for the eyes of my Soul,
Where did You go?
Come, come, so the water
Will spring from our oven.

Come, so the barren land will be green,
The cemeteries will become a garden,
Grapes will ripen,
And our bread will be baked.

O sun of Soul, sun of Heart,
O Beauty who shames the sun with His beauty,
Come and see how this sticky mud
Got stuck to our Soul.
We can't get rid of it.

The kindness of Your face
Has changed so many thorns
Into so many rose gardens
That our faith has been acknowledged
Hundreds of thousands of times.

O eternal Love, in order to deliver our Soul
Out of this dungeon to God,
How beautifully You show Your face
From behind this mold.

O our bright morning,
Make joy during the time of gloom.
Show in the evening
A bright, wonderful day.

You make pearls out of blue beads.
You scare Venus.
You make kings out of the penniless.
Good for You, our Sultan.

Where are the eyes
That can see a trace of Your dust?
Where are the ears
That hear our testament?
Where is the mind
That understands our evidence?

If the Heart sees the beauty of that sugar cane
And tells of its grace and favors,
Taste and flavor will sing songs
At the bottom of our every tooth.

The sound of drums coming from the land of Soul
Says, "Particles are reaching wholeness,
Sweet basil to sweet basil, rose to rose.
Everything is becoming free
From the jail of our thorns."

8.

O rainy season, like sad lovers
Crying because of the absence
Of our beloved ones,
Pour your rain on our friends.

O eyes of the clouds,
Pour your tears out of cups,
Because you are jealous of our Beauties,
The Ones with faces like the moon.

Look at the crying of this cloud.
Look at the smile of this garden.
Now our patients get well
And are saved
From their father's cries and begging.

This cloud which rains continuously
Resembles God's blessing
To the thirsty, chapped-lipped friends.
God is the One who offers this huge jar to rinds.[23]

The sky is spreading pearls
Over the barren plains of earth
Which lost their harvest
Because of our deceitful Beauty's failure
To give provisions.

This cloud is like Jacob.
The rose in the garden is Joseph.
Josephs are smiling
Because of our crying clouds.

One drop becomes pearl,
The other, narcissus.
The hands of the ones
Who make a living on the plains by crops
Are filled with goods and blessings.

The garden and meadow that offer wines
Were decorated with flowers yesterday,
Because our men who are fond of wine
Drank it on an empty stomach.

Close your mouth like an oyster.
Don't bring your drunkenness
In front of the naive,
So that our knowledgeable friends
Will come back from the land of Absence.

9.

Ⓞ Heart, what excuses have you given
For all these faults?
Loyalties come from Him;
From you, all these troubles.

Kindness comes from Him;
From you, all this nonsense.
Favors come from Him;
From you, these mistakes.

Benevolence, goodness, gifts
Come from Him;
From you, this jealousy,
These bad thoughts and surmises.

Why so many favors?
So your bitter Soul
Can become better and sweeter.
Why is He pulling you to Himself?
So you can reach the Ones
Who have attained the truth.

The moment you repent your faults
And start calling Him,
That's the moment He pulls you to Himself
And gets you out of trouble.

When you're afraid of the sin you've committed,
Of asking for His help to get out of it,
Then, right then, why don't you see the one
Who scares you inside of yourself?

In His hands you are like a small crystal ball.
He rolls you, then covers you
And throws you in the air
Just to be amused.

Sometimes He leaves you to your own nature,
The way you were born.
You fall in love with gold, silver
And the love of women.
But sometimes He shines on you
With the light of Mustafâ's[24] image,
So that you'll be illuminated.

When He pulls you this way,
You join with good people.
When He pulls you that way,
You mix with bad people.
He either passes your ship
Through this turbulence
Or breaks and wrecks it.

Pray, pray secretly,
Cry, moan and groan so much through the night
That a voice will come to your ear
From the seven layers of sky.

At last at dawn, a voice came to Shuayb's[25] ear
After he yelled and cried and cried
And shed tears like the dew.

"I'll pardon you if you're guilty,
Forgive your sins.
If you want the heaven I give you,
Stop this praying and be silent."

Shuayb said, "I don't want this or that.
Clearly, I want to see the beauty of God.
To reach Him, even if the seven seas
Become fire,
I will plunge in and pass through them.

"If you expel me from Your temple,
Deprive me of that Beauty,
If my wet eyes don't see that Beauty,
I might as well stay in hell.
Heaven is not for me."

"At least, don't cry so much," they said.
"When you cry so much,
Your eyes lose their sight."

"If, at the end, both my eyes see Him,
Why should I worry about becoming blind?
My every particle will turn into eyes.

"If my eyes are deprived of seeing Him,
If they don't deserve the Beloved,
Let them become blind."

In this world, everyone gives life
For his own beloved.
One beloved is a bag of blood,
The other is sunlight.

Since everyone chooses a beloved, good or bad,
Isn't it sad for us
To become nothing for nothing?

One day on the road
Someone became a companion to Beyazid.[26]
Beyazid asked, "O bad man, what do you do?"

The man said, "I ride a donkey.
I've become a slave to the donkey."
Beyazid said, "Go away," then said,
"My God, kill this man's donkey
So that he can become a slave to God."

10.

O Joseph, whose name is beautiful,
How nicely you walk on our roof!
O the One who breaks our glass!
O the One who tears open our trap!

O our light, our wedding, our assembly!
O our kingdom!
Boil our bitter water.
Ferment our grapes
That they may become wine.

O our charmer, our desire,
Our Kible,[27] our God,
You throw our aloe wood on the fire.
Now watch the smoke.

O our deceitful Beloved, O our friend,
The One who set a trap for our drunken Heart,
Don't go away.
Pawn our turban.

The feet of Heart got stuck in the mud.
Never mind Heart.
I am giving Soul to Him, Soul.
Alas to Heart for the Love in which Heart fell.
Alas to us.

11.

O One who sweetens our Soul,
The one by himself, make him go beyond,
And the one beyond,
Make him come back to his senses.
Give something to the poor.

Do favors for Lovers.
Lighten the daybreak.
Turn the antidote to poison.
Give something to the poor.

Look at us with Your face like a moon.
With kindness You search for the poor.
Give us mercy, make us Your companion.
Give something to the poor.

You give the sense of Love to the Soul
With Your Grace, like the moon.
How have You come into our company?
Give something to the poor.

What is the sign of the dervish?
A Soul sprinkles pearls,
A tongue sprinkles pearls,
Not a mantle made with hundreds of patches.
Give something to the poor.

You are Adam and, at the same time,
Jesus and Mary.
You are the secret and, at the same time,
The One who knows the secret.
Give something to the poor.

Bitter becomes sweet with You.
Blasphemy becomes faith with You.
Thorns change to the roses of August.
Give something to the poor.

O my Soul, my Beloved,
My blasphemy, my religion,
Give something to the poor.

O one who falls into grief,
The one who worships the body,
Don't struggle with flesh.
Don't fight with Soul.
Don't look at the body.
Don't look at me.
Give something to the poor.

O my Light, I'll do something today.
I'll turn around Your spiritual light,
Then I'll give life to Love.
Give something to the poor.

Are You the One who is looking to blame us?
Are You a snake or a fish?
Will You tell who You are?
Give something to the poor.

My Beautiful, You can't be You
And, at the same time, Him.
This is not the way for You.
Throw this Soul to Absence.
Give something to the poor.

12.

O Joseph, at last come to this Jacob
Who has become blind.
O hidden Jesus,
Appear from the dome of this sky.

My Heart is darkened because of separation.
My Heart was like a bow string
Now turned into hair.
Poor Jacob has become old.
O young Joseph, come.

O Moses, son of Imran,
I have such Mount Sinais
In my Heart for you.
Come now from Mount Sinai.
They're worshiping the oxen as a god.

The pale color of my face is like saffron.
My bent neck has turned into a harp.
I have been tightened and squeezed
In the grave of my body.
Come, O Soul, give cheer and spaciousness.

My eyes, which watch Muhammad, tell You
That I have been longing with grief for You.
O Secret of the verse,
"We send you to the universes
To show God's compassion!" [28]
Show Your face through that scattered hair.
Come!

The sun is like a sunset in front of You.
O One who grabs the reward from the King!
O the eye which looks with God, sees with God!
O the Heart which knows everything! Come!

All Souls are like body for You.
You are the Soul.
What's the good of a body without Soul?
I've given You my Heart for a long time.
Come, O Beloved, I'll give You my Soul, too.

The crops of my Soul have been harvested
Since You took my Heart.
The last trouble is You. Go.
The last cure is You. Come.

O Beloved, my medicine is You.
My remedy is You.
The light of my Heart
Which has been broken into a hundred pieces
Is You.
Everything in this helpless Heart except You
Has gone. Come.

I have not been able to appreciate You.
Destiny tells me:
"Wound your Heart with arrows.
Break your head with stones. Come."

O One whose level is stated in the verse,
"The distance between them
Is only two arrow throws,"[29]
O One who has an exalted state,
O my Sultan,
No one could be Your confidant.
Come from the level of
"Maybe it is much closer." [30]

O Sultan as beautiful as the moon!
O One more beautiful
Than a hundred beauties!
O water, O fire, come!
Come, O pearls. Come, O sea!

O One to whom my Soul
Has become a slave and servant,
O Shemseddin, O my Archangel Gabriel,
Because of You,
Tebriz became the mounted throne of God.
Come from Mescid-i Aksâ.[31]

13.

O Spring of the Lover,
The green has been made pregnant by you.
O One who makes the garden and meadow smile,
Do you have any news
From our Beloved?

O winds which have the cleanest breath,
O One who comes
To help the wailing Lovers,
O breeze which is purer than Soul and space,
Where were you then?
Where were you?

O mischievous one from the land of Rum,
O deceitful one from the land of Ethiopia,
I am confused.
This beautiful smell is either
From the skirt of Joseph
Or the mantle of Muhammad.

O river of truth,
You are flowing in our Beloved's canal.
You are the Mount Sinai of the Heart.
You add Soul to Souls.

O Charmer whose manners are pleasant,
His essence, His worlds are beautiful.
O Friend to whom month and year
Have become slaves,
Your months, Your years are beautiful.

14.

Verse 197

O suddenly-risen uproar!
O endless compassion!
O fire which sets the forest of thought ablaze!

Today You came with a smile
Like the key to the dungeon.
You came like God's favor to the needy.

You are the doorkeeper of the sun.
You are the One for whom to be hoped,
The One to be depended upon.
You are the One to be desired
And the One who desires.
You are the beginning; You are the end.

You appear in hearts and adorn the mind.
You make wishes and, at the same time,
Make wishes come true.

O peerless One who gives gratis to the Soul!
O the taste and flavor of knowledge
And the pleasure of keeping that knowledge,
All except You is a fake and an excuse.
Everything else is an illness.
You are the remedy.

We fall in the trap and become cross-eyed.
Without sin, we face all kinds of grudges.
Sometimes we become drunk
With black-eyed Houris;[32]
Other times, we 're fond of soups and breads.

See this drunkenness
And leave the mind behind you.
Watch only this snack. Forget the other.
It's not worth even one piece of bread and a meal
To jump into this adventure.

That invisible Master puts you to work.
You take hundreds
Of different-colored precautions,
Reach the brightness and fall into darkness.
In between, you keep struggling.

O my brave man, pull the ears of Soul secretly.
Pray to God with all your Heart and Soul
So you can stay away from people.
I swear to God, they all are nonsense.

Be silent! I have urgent things to do.
I'll get under the flag.
Throw away the paper. Break the pen.
Here is the Cupbearer, coming, coming.

15.

A word came from sky to Soul:
"It's time. Come back."
Soul answered, "Greetings,
O Beauty who invites me.
I'm coming."

"With pleasure," Soul continued.
"I'll give hundreds of Souls for You.
Call me back once more
So I can reach the state of a Hel-etâ." [33]

O peerless guest, You took away
The patience and decisions of our Soul.
Where should I search for You?
Where can I find You?
"Beyond Soul, beyond places," He answered.

I'll untie the heavy chains
Of those in the dungeon
And put a ladder to the sky
So Soul will ascend.

Your beauty adds Soul to Souls.
You are from our town.
Even so, why are you favoring strangers?
Is this fair to your friends?

You drank vagrancy like a syrup
And forgot the way home.
That woman, that witch of Kabil,
Has cast many spells upon you.

Why don't you feel dizzy?
Don't you get that urge in your Heart
When all these caravans
Are going there one after the other?

Haven't you heard
The caravan Master and the sound of bells
Ringing from front to back?
There are so many friends waiting for us.

So many people are waiting for us.
All of them are our drunks.
Thinking of us, they passed out of themselves.
They are yelling in our ears,
"O poor ones, come to the side of the Sultan."

16.

*L*ook at His beauty. Watch His manner,
That figure, that stature,
That face, those eyes.
Look at His hands and feet.
Watch His color,
That dignity, that calmness.
Watch that One dressed
Like a full moon.

Shall I start with the cypress,
Or tell about the tulips,
Or describe the jasmine?
Shall I talk about the candle and bowl,
Or the roses that dance in the morning breeze?

Love looks like a pulpit for fireworks,
Dressed to become the form
Which came and cut the road
For the caravan of Heart.
O young one, give a moment of mercy.

All night I've been in the fire,
Burning until morning.
I'm so bright and happy from the morning sun.

I've been turning around His face
Which resembles the Moon.
I send greetings to Him
Without lips or tongue.
I throw myself to the ground
Before He invites me in.

You are the rose garden of the earth
And the eyes and light of the universe.
Yet when You step into the land of cruelty,
You become all the sorrow and grief of the world.

I come to Your temple to sacrifice my life.
"Don't give me trouble, go away," You say.
I return to serve You.
"Oh, stupid one, where are you?" You say.

Your reflection is having an affair
With a fiery Lover.
I hope my eye won't lose sight of Your face
For even one moment.

O Heart, what has happened
To your patience, your decision?
Where is your work, your occupation?
Why do you lose your sleep day and night?

Heart, expound upon the beauty of Your face
And praise those charming
Narcissus eyes of Yours.
Talk about that hair which looks like hyacinth,
Those beautiful eyebrows
And those ruby-colored lips
That tell such fascinating stories.

O Love, You have many different names
Among the people.
But yesterday I gave You yet another name.
I call You
Pain which has no remedy.

O Beautiful, my Soul is enlightened by You.
I whirl around like the sky because of You,
My Soul, my Beauty.
Send some wheat
So that the mill won't become confused.

I won't talk about Him anymore.
After this verse, I'll be silent.
It's enough.
My Soul has been burned by this desire.
My God, You take good care of us.

17.

Ⓞ our Joseph, Your name is so beautiful.
You climb our roof so nicely.
We've opened the door.
Come down from the roof
And enter through the door.

O my ocean full of coral,
I swear in God's name
That my anxious Soul has no patience.
Its head is so dizzy
From the rolling of this mill.

Caravan Master, for my sake,
For God's sake, don't move the caravan
Out of this place.
Don't go away. Let the camels rest here.

No, no, go insane one. Go like a madman.
Walk nicely in the blood.
Don't talk about what or how.
Walk without what, without how,
Because there is no resting place for the Soul.

When your body goes into the ground,
Your Soul rises to the sky.
Don't worry if your mantle is torn.
There is no end for your Soul.

You're not a stranger
To the secrets of Heart.
Show your face because you are a mirror.
And because you've fallen in Love,
You will certainly go through
Many trials and much turbulence.

You ask me,
"How and where are you going,
Running carelessly like that?
Be careful! You're sailing through blood.
How far do you plan to go?
You're not telling me."

I answer, "You're going through the fire of Heart,
Jumping over the hearts
That are spread over the ground,
Rolling with the Love of Heart
Until you reach the sea of
'God does whatever He desires.' "[34]

Every moment an envoy comes,
Grabs the Soul by his neck and pulls.
Every moment an image appears.
They all tell the Soul,
"Come back to your own source."

The Heart is running away
From this world of color and smell
By yelling and screaming,
"Where is that source? Where is that origin?"

18.

$\mathcal{I}$ have seen the Beloved.
I have seen that Beauty today,
The One who gives light
To every action, every force.
His glory was shining in the sky
Like the Soul of Muhammad.

The sun was ashamed after seeing His face.
The sky split open and fragmented like a Heart.
Water and ground became brighter than fire
Just from His sparks.

"Show me," I said,
"Show me the stairs so I can ascend the sky."
He answered, "The stair is your head.
Put your head under your feet."

When you put your feet over your head,
You step on the stars.
If you overcome your fancies and pleasures,
You step on air.
Why don't you come?

Hundreds of roads become apparent to you.
Every dawn you ascend the sky like prayers.

19.

O our friend, our Beloved,
Our confidant, our Joseph,
The light of our bazaar and our demand!

Look! Last year fell in Love
With our present time.
We are all spendthrifts.
You are hundreds of treasures to us,
Hundreds of our spent monies.

We are lazy.
You are hundreds of pilgrimages,
Hundreds of businesses and occupations.
We fall asleep.
You are hundreds of states of awakeness.

We are the sick ones.
You are hundreds of salves for our wounds.
We are all ruined.
Your kindness, your favor
Is our architect.

I said yesterday to Love,
"O our crafty Sultan of Sultans,
Don't deny that You hid our turban."

He answered me by saying,
"No, what We do comes from you,
Because Our mountain echoes your voice to you."

"Yes," I said, "true. We are the mountain.
This is our voice.
But, O Friend who does what He wishes,
The same is not true for us.
We cannot do what we wish."

20.[35]

Our feast, our wedding
Will be auspicious to the world.
God fit the feast and wedding
To our length like a proper garment.

Venus and the moon
Will be matched to each other,
The parrot with sugar.
The most beautifully-faced Beloved
Makes a different kind of wedding every night.

With the favor of our Sultan's prosperity,
Hearts become spacious
And men pair up with each other.
Troubles and anxieties are all gone.

Here tonight, You go again
To the wedding and feasting.
O Beauty who adorned our city,
You will be groom to the beauties.

How nicely You walk in our neighborhood,
Coming to us so beautifully.
O our river, O One
Who is searching for us,
How nicely You flow in our stream.

How nicely You flow with our desires,
Unfastening the binding of our feet.
You make us walk so nicely, holding our hand,
O Joseph of our world.

Cruelty suits You well.
It's a mistake for us to expect Your loyalty.
Step as You wish on our bloody Soul.

O Soul of my Soul, pull our Souls
To our Beloved's temple.
Take this piece of bone.
Give it as a gift to our Huma.[36]

O wise ones, give thanks
To our Sultan's kindness, who adds Souls to Soul,
Keep dancing, O considerate ones.
Keep whirling and dancing.

At the wedding night of rose and Nesrin[37]
I hang the drum on my neck.
Tonight, the tambourine and small drum
Will become our clothes.

Be silent! Venus becomes the Cupbearer tonight
And offers glasses to our sweetheart,
Whose skin is fair and rosy,
Who takes a glass and drinks.

For the sake of God, because of our praying,
Now sufis become exuberant
At the assembly of God's Absence.
They put the belt of zeal on their waists
And start Sema.[38]

One group of people froth like the sea,
Prostrating like waves.
The other group battles like swords,
Drinking the blood of our glasses.

Be silent! Tonight, the Sultan
Went to the kitchen.
He is cooking with joy.
But a most unusual thing,
Tonight, the Beloved is cooking our Halva.[39]

21.

O angel of death, afraid of us,
Afraid of our battle,
Afraid because you can't wear our colors,
You can't.

If you get in a fight with us,
If you dare to challenge us,
None of your vessels will remain intact
Because of the wounds
That will be inflicted by His soldiers.

First you have to drink wine.
You must get so drunk
That you pass out of yourself.
Then you might join our harmony.

If you want to drink this wine,
First you must squeeze like a bottle.
When you become a bottle,
Hit yourself on our stone,
Hit yourself on our stone.

Whoever drinks that red wine
Grows and attains his desire,
Reaches pleasure from our squeezed Heart.

Our doorkeeper plays many two-stringed lutes
And six-stringed berbad[40] in that river.
Whoever drinks will rub shoulders with Sultans.

Here even time's Mars is female
At the strike of this dagger.
No one comes with a headscarf to our fight.
No one comes with a scarf to our battle.

If you want an arrow from the sun,
You should get a shield from the full moon.
If you are a Caesar, walk.
Pass through our light,
Pass through our light.

If we slaughter you,
Become Isaac for us.
Plunge in our ocean and be silenced.
Be silent so that
Our power won't destroy your boat,
Won't destroy your boat.

22.

𝓙 sit at Your door
Hoping Your generosity, Your blessing
Might open it and invite me in.

O Beautiful, the One
On whose face hundreds of sparks
Of mercy's light and kindness shine,
My Soul is overwhelmed at Your door
From the smell of musk and ambergris.

We are drunk. Our heads are dizzy.
We have nothing to do with others' business.
We don't even care if the world
Turns upside down,
As long as Your Love lasts forever.

Your Love claps its hands,
Creating new universes, new centuries
Beyond the sky, out of the great emptiness.

O Love, smile like a rose.
O One whose looks are similar
To that beautiful universal intelligence,
O peerless rider of the land of Hel-eta,[41]
Catch the sun. Put it into a sack.

We are Your guest today.
We are the drunk of Your smiling face.
I swear to God, my Heart leaves me
Once I mention Your face.

Is there any roof besides Yours?
Any name besides Your name?
O sweet, beautifully-mannered Cupbearer,
There is no cup but Yours.

I will grab him and beg for his help
If I find an awakened Soul.
I wish I could sleep
So that I could see Your face in a dream.

O great man, slaves, people
Are gathered at Your door.
Get out, stagger along.
I am out of myself. I am drunk
Because of Heart-catching, drunken eyes.

See the bloody tears, the hundreds of torn shirts
By Your grief.
Listen to all the yelling and screaming.
Look at the blood of my lungs
Smeared all over my face, my back, my front.

The one who sees Your face
Runs from town to town and becomes mad.
Why should I curse him,
Want him to face all that trouble?
He is going to eat stones and soil anyway.

The very worst comes to the one
Who doesn't know You.
O Sultan of mankind,
Don't prevent me from seeing You.
Don't make me blind.

The blood runs like a torrent
To the shore of the sea of Soul.
It merges with the sea.
The ones who know the sea
Forget everything else.

One astonished river runs smoothly;
Another one is lost.
The first one thanks God;
The other prays for help.
"God is the only One
Able to change one condition to the other." [42]

O One who rises like a sun
And falls in Love with the poor,
Please do a favor for Your people.

The rose has passed out of himself
After seeing You,
Suddenly torn his dress and petals to pieces.
The harp begins to cry after hearing Your harp,
And bends its head down in shame.

Venus doesn't have a better song than Yours.
What kind of flute could she play?
She puts her lips to Yours
To learn new tunes.

With just a little hope
All the sugar canes keep swaying.
You give the kingdom to whomever You please. [43]
They also want to rise.

The harp is no good without You.
The reed flute is engulfed in grief.
Take one in Your arms. Kiss the other.
The tambourine says, "Hit, hit my face
So I may become more valuable."

Make this Heart,
Which has broken to pieces
And been scattered around,
Well drunk, so that it can find today
The things it lost yesterday.

O great Sultan, from now on,
It's a pity to stay sober.
I made an oath to God
That I would not mention Him
When I'm sober.

Don't bring any more proof.
Either give wine or talk.
Like one who found You through Grace,
Follow the adventure of the sufi.

23.

Who cares if death comes
And grabs my being?
I'll welcome death.
If I have hundreds of lives, I'll give them all.

I'll ascend first to the sky,
Then with joy to the land of Nothingness.
I'll tell the Master of the house,
"You took away all my patience, all my decisions.
You should have come sooner."

You snatch the stars from the moon
And carry them off piece by piece.
Sometimes you take away the baby sucking milk.
Sometimes you take away the nanny.

I have a Heart like the earth.
It pulls huge mountains.
Why should I be loaded with straw?
I am a man who moves mountains.
Save me from this barn.

Every hair in my body has become a lion.
But I'm tired of dead wishes.
I am flour, not grain.
Why did I come to the mill?

Grain was born from an ear of corn
And goes to the mill.
Yet I am not the son of an ear of corn.
I was born from the moon.
My place is not the mill.

No, no, moonlight also reflects the mill
Through the window.
But it returns to the moon,
Not the bakery store.

If I were a friend,
With my mind I would tell you more.
But be silent now
So that the wind in the air
Won't hear this fable.

24.

$\mathfrak{I}$ love You with all my Heart and Soul.
That's my sin.
Why do You turn Your face
From my pale saffron face?

Either take care of this bleeding Heart
Or give the patience of
"God does whatever He desires." [44]

We came to the crossroads after a long walk.
One road was 'Be patient.'
The other was 'Give thanks for the blessing.'
But I can't see either one
Without the light of Your face.

No water flows in any canal
When You turn Your face away.
Particles don't appear
If the sun doesn't rise at early dawn.

The Hearts of beauties can't be dizzy and drunk
Without Your wine.
How can the devil run from Lâhavle[45]
If You don't protect us?

If You don't add a palmful of Helie[46]
To the medicine with Your own hand,
It can be neither pill nor paste.

Without the uproars of Your clouds,
The sun doesn't enter the sign of the lion.
Without You, no artery pulsates
In the hands and feet of the devout.

You hide meaning in death,
Awakeness in sleep.
You get spring water from stone.
You manifest faithfulness in lightning.

The dark torrent of the night
Carries away mind and intelligence everywhere.
Who better to bring them back
Than the follower of Hel-etâ?[47]

O Soul of the whole or Soul of the part!
O the One who provides a dress
To cover the garden and meadow!
O the One who invites Soul with the drumbeat,
Chanting, "Come, O wandering Soul!"

Everyone wants to cheat
And take Oshur[48] from me.
But I don't have the mind
To understand this word.

From wherever understanding comes,
One has to go in that direction.
Whoever makes your life longer,
Pray for him to have a long life.

The One who squeezes your Heart,
The One who makes you green and grow,
Gives the color of rose to your face.
He is the One who forces you to pray
And accepts your praying,
Grants your prayers.

He adds *R* to be,
Nun to *elif*[49]
In order to say the word Rabbena,[50]
Which gives breath and power to your mouth.

I follow Your orders, saying,
"Lebbeyk, Lebbeyk," [51]
O munificent One.
With Your Love in my Heart,
I keep turning like a millstone.

The millstone turns and turns,
But the mill doesn't understand
That our nourishment comes from that.
So does the miller's income.

Water is the one that turns the stone.
When God stops the water, nothing moves.

Be silent. All these words
Are coming from our secret.
You be silent, so that the One
Who doesn't slip in His talk can tell.

25.

I should wail.
I should do so much that, in the end,
I would clean the rust off the mirror
Of the disbeliever's Heart.

The Heart is riding
The horse of Your Love.
Your Love's horse is so fast
That every step
Is passing the land of Soul by miles.

If You show Your bright ruby lips
In spite of all the darkness,
Hard rocks will rain from the sky
On the Hearts of the stone-hearted ones.

Do You know why they deny such brightness?
They see the splendid glory,
But are ashamed of themselves.
They're jealous of You.

If that isn't really the case,
Even though they're blind now,
Their eyes will be opened eventually,
And they will see thousands of beauties,
Of moon-pieces like stars
Clustered on the side.

The joy of Your glory
Opens the eyes of the blind.
The beauty of Your roads
Causes the lame to walk.

Even though they walk,
They still lose themselves suddenly on the road.
In fact, every mind that grows in Your garden,
Follows that air.

I've seen so many people,
Their insides empty, wailing like a flute.
For that reason, many brave necks
Are bent by grief like a harp.

For that reason, so many caravans
Are lost on the road.
For that reason, so many ships
Are wrecked and run aground.

All those broken and ruined ones,
With their Hearts and Souls,
Keep their hopes pinned on You,
Expecting to get something
From Your endless knowledge.

It is expected that Your favor,
Which is the favor of favors,
Will alleviate suffering.
Every place will turn into peace
And be done with struggling.

It is expected that this humdrum world
Will stop.
It will be a different road and journey.
New melodies will appear in every Heart,
And Hearts will be attached
To each other like chains.

With the beautiful invitation
Of Shems of Tebriz,
Every particle would rise
And ascend to the sky,
Every hair would become a brave.

26.

Ⓞ Sultan of Sultans, blood never sleeps.
O beautiful Moon face,
A sea of blood comes from trouble and grief,
Boiling, flowing over my eyes.
How could sleep possibly get there?

If I closed my lips,
My Heart would overflow.
When I pour water on it,
It boils and rises more.

If people don't condone my Love
And criticize me, I understand.
But how can an accused one
Ever reach light and glory?

My blood overflows, becomes words in my mouth,
Then drops out of my pen.
The alphabet goes to Solomon
Like ants begging.

O Solomon, O Sultan,
O the One who grants favors,
Your favors exalt every goodness.
Souls are the shells for Your pearl.
Grasses are the hearts in Your garden.

We are a helpless bunch of ants,
Separated from the place of harvest,
Wandering from one side to the other.
Come and help us.

We are a handful of dirt in Your hand,
Your slave and Your servant.
Even with all this blindness,
We can see and watch the Beauties.

Don't look at us.
Remember Your kindness.
"He doesn't need anything.
Everything needs Him."[52]
As You praise Yourself,
You may forgive the one
Who did all the sinning,
Committed bad deeds in both worlds.

O warmth of greatness,
O Beautiful, Heart has seen You.
Give him an alm.
How can I see anything else in this world?
How can I watch anything else in the sky?

The Heart has drunk wine
From the Sultan of Sultans.
If such a Heart were to drink,
Even from the clean, pure Fountain of Life,
It would stick in its throat.

To the One who sees that Beauty
Who is bright like a moon in beauty and charm,
The sun is seen as a dark annoyance
Resembling only a small spark in His eye.

To the Lovers who have been separated
From that beautiful Sultan
Who has not been extolled,
Despite hundreds of honors,
Their sweet life becomes sandy, sour.

O Soul, cut the words short.
While you're talking,
Try to go as far as Tebriz,
To the way of the Sultan of Sultans.

O flesh, don't be lazy like a dog.
Don't try to bark.
Give up your being
In order to go toward the Sultan of beings.

O beautiful One, hundreds of existences
Are nothing but a handful of dust.
Hundreds of Sultans of Sultans are nothing
But servants at His side.
O Charmer to whom hundreds of Âsafs[53]
Turn into slaves,
Even Solomon becomes astonished with His Love.

Solomon felt he would fall
Into all kinds of tricks because of that Love,
Would go through lots of trouble.
He started trembling because he knew
All these exaltations would degrade him.

Suddenly a devilish trick came.
A glass of loftiness and fame inflated his ego
And took his greatness away.

That peerless Sultan at one time worried
About his belongings.
He put giant fairies
Row upon row to protect himself.[54]

He then realized he had fallen
Into a trap of his desire and fancy,
Turned his back on those gardens
And understood that all his belongings
Actually did not belong to him.

He had cut the neck of the giant fairies' necks
With the sword of distress,
Because they kept him away
From the Beloved on the other side.

At once, the grace of Shemseddin,
To whom everyone is a slave and servant,
Rose like a moon and said,
"O choice man,
Don't burn and hurt the universe."

When he heard that order from the Sultan,
He prostrated himself.
He received such assurance from Tebriz
That he would gladly sacrifice both worlds.

27.

𝔍 don't know how much I should cry and moan
To make the Beloved feel sorry for me,
How much blood these eyes should shed
So I can see the rose garden.

When the sun shines,
I don't complain that much about separation.
But if the Heart would show me a new road,
I would start all over again.

O universal mind
Which has all these skills,
Teach me a spell,
A way for me to go
So that the beauty of the beautiful Beloved
Will have pity on me.

The Heart cannot find the light
Of Çigil's[55] candle,
Is unable to reach that Glory.
One is water; the other is dirt.
How could water and dirt understand
The desire of this deceitful Beauty's Heart?

The Archangel Gabriel
Is understanding and tolerant.
But how can he know
The taste of well-fed suckling calf meat?
How can one hunt the beautiful phoenix
With a trap of grain?

Even a small fly looks like a phoenix
In front of a phoenix who has been trapped.
O mind which resembles a spider,
How long will you keep making this web?

Where is Jesus, whose breath is so holy
That even without the means of Mary
He would be so exalted, so overflowing,
That the Christians' Hearts would become untied
And throw off their Zünnâr? [56]

Deccâl[57] of grief
Who looks like fire
And burns everything like fire,
Who lays a carpet of fire,
Where is Jesus
Who will draw a knife on that Deccal?

All the health and soundness
Which comes to the body
Comes from You.
The uproar which comes to the Soul
Comes from You.
The signs of Jesus' return
Before the Last Day of Judgement
Also come from You.

Once a stone is thrown at glass,
It falls down because of its sorrow.
The thorn would feel as if it were on fire
If it didn't have the rose.

I became like Vâmik,
Who is separated from Azrâ,[55]
Because I didn't deserve Him.
But even then, in the Lover's Heart,
There still is Love's drunkenness, dizziness.

As in a stately game of chess,
Wherein a hundred Souls
Provide provisions for the Shah,
He puts hundreds of mountains
On top of one straw.
For the one who suffers one grief,
He gives a hundred times
More grief and calamities.

I see the Soul has reached the Sultan,
Passed beyond himself, separated from self.
With the Sultan's favor,
He has made the window and door for Soul.

It is possible that the great Sultan
With innumerable favors
Would exempt us from the custom
Of asking forgiveness for those sins.

The Soul who turns to Him
Will become like Bâyezîd,[59]
Or turn his face to Senâî[60]
Or give perfumes to Attâr.[61]

The Beloved in whose temple the Soul is served
Is such a Beloved
That even days are drunk
After drinking from His glasses.
Once you mention His name,
You'll have to repeat it again and again.

He is the great Sultan Shemseddin.
Because of Him,
Tebriz became the land of Soul,
Filled with lights like Arsh.[62]
All the halos are jealous of His luminous lighting.

Hundreds of thousands bravo the moment
When Archangel Gabriel will reveal His secrets.
Hundreds of thousands bravo this holiest
Of His holy hour.

You sit at His Love assembly
Without affection and hatred
And see that the curtain
Has been put up and secured
With hundreds of nails
So that the disbeliever cannot see through.

28.

At dawn, I saw that Sultan
At the main street of Hel-etâ.[63]
He was in the sleep of heedlessness.
He did not know about Abû-Alî[64] or Abu-l Alâ.[65]

I filled a cup from the wine
Which made my head dizzy
And put it in front of him.
"Come, my Sultan," I said, "drink."

"O so-and-so," he said, "what's this?"
"That is the blood of Lovers," I said.
"On top of the fire of Love,
It became pure like Soul."

"Since you drank, you've become exuberant
At the cup of Soul,
At the garden and meadow
Of the secrets of God," he said.
"I will drink that wine."

My drunk Beloved took the glass from my hand
And drank the wine
Which adds Soul to Soul-like Souls.

He passed the Soul in joy and cheer
Hundreds of times.
The sky said that now evil eyes
Won't stay away from You.

29.

The Cupbearer offers lots of wine,
Offers that hope and fear will both disappear.
Cut the neck of thought!
Where are we?
Where is He?

Bring the cup. Give us more and more wine.
Pull our mind up from the roots.
Untie the daily struggle which barely covers
His face and wide open pleasure
From existence.

Come to the assembly as a drunk.
Take the veil from your face.
O the secret of
"God does whatever He desires,"[66]
Come as you did before.

See those tired, scattered insane Ones?
See the Ones who've freed themselves
From the ties of existence?
Watch the Ones who fall in Love with Love.
That's when trouble starts.

Come even faster. Put your senses in your mind.
It's getting late.
My Heart is tired and sick of this town.
Make Him drunk and save Him,
Again saying, "Come fast. Come."

Take this rope from my hands
And tie the feet of Abu-l Hasan.[67]
Offer me a glass so I can lose my head and feet.

Among every-day events,
In the gossip of every moment,
The one who keeps talking
About the subjects of Abu-l Alâ,[68]
Abu-l Alâ is simply absurd.

Don't give water and bread.
Don't give peace and sleep, O Beautiful.
To the thirst of His Love,
The blood of hundreds like us would be sacrificed.

I'm Your guest today.
I'm Your drunk.
I'm all over the place today.
That news is spread over the entire city.
Everyone knows it.
Today is the day of drink.
Come all, come.

If anyone is looking for any purchaser
Other than God,
He is nothing but a donkey.
He's searching for something to eat
Like a donkey at the green of that stock hole.

Be advised that the green
Which grows around the stock hole
Makes your mouth and beard smell bad.
As Muhammad said, "Stay away from the rushes
And the green around the sewage,
Because it makes your mouth and beard
Smell bad." [69]

I am away from the green
Which grows around the sewage,
I am away
From the beauties of garden and meadow.
I am away from pride, free from self.
I am drunk with the divine wine.

How the moon appears above the horizon!
How the rose appears among the grasses!
That is how, suddenly, the image of a Beauty
Appeared in the Heart.

All earthly images
Start running toward His image,
Just like pieces of iron
Run toward a magnet.

Rubies are like stones in front of Him.
Lions are wild donkeys,
Swords are like shields,
And the sun is a bunch of particles.

The earth became Mount Sinai.
Every part was shining.
The Soul, like Moses,
Lost his mind and passed out
Because of manifestation.

Every drunk is at a different world of union,
Merges with His Source of Source.
Absence beats time in the timelessness.
He claps His hands openly.

Every blade of grass is green.
Every particle is yelling,
"Patience is the key to grief;
Gratitude is the key to contention."

The rose says to the Nightingale,
"O One to whom hundreds like me
Will be sacrificed,
You were a guard. You've now become King.
How long will you keep saying,
'May you live long'?"

While praying and crying,
Lightning struck every needy particle
With such confusion
That they forgot praying.

For peace is the way to wish.
Mildness is the stair of joy.
Fire is a good judge for gold.
Glory is the judge for Love.

Love is the light of nights.
Separation prepares, matures for union.
O One who walks on my chest,
Union is the antidote for separation.

The sun is one of our horses.
The full moon is one of our guards.
Love is one of our close friends
With whom we hang around.
Who knows what we have in our head?
Who knows?

O one who is asking me about His Love,
You honor Him. Be grateful for Him.
Because once He appears,
All the wishes and desires about Him
Will be scattered like particles.

O one who is asking for my story,
I have a share of Love,
But drunkenness eradicates my trouble.
What fortune and happiness for me!

Growing, spreading because of your apples,[70]
Our mornings are the cause of pulling together.
A Soul is from Your Soul.
There is hope and begging
Turning from one state to another,
Changing from hand to hand.

The wind coming from You
Gives light to the eyes,
Makes blind Jacob see again.
Our Joseph among the people
Becomes generous with the things God sells.

The sun, moon and eleven stars
Prostrate themselves
And fall in front of You to worship,
Whereas Joseph saw this
When he had a short sleep.

O the one who keeps complaining
Either because of Love
Or the sharp nails of separation,
Be aware that all this favor and goodness
Is our gain
And the things people spend
Are our goodness and favor.

30.

Who am I that I could listen to advice,
  O Cupbearer?
Turn the wine glasses, O Cupbearer.
Pour the wine for our Soul
Which adds Soul to our Soul, O Cupbearer.

O Cupbearer who holds Lovers by their hands,
The One who helps Lovers,
Give the glass of Soul to my hand.
Keep it away from the stranger's lips.
Offer it to me secretly.

Give the bread to bread eaters.
Give the loaf of bread
To those greedy, helpless ones.
Bread's lovers
Don't deserve Your treasure, O Cupbearer.

O the One who becomes Soul to the Soul of Soul,
We didn't come here to eat bread.
Jump. Get up. Don't put on a poor face
At the assembly of the Sultan.

Just take this big glass
And offer it to that old man.
Once the old man of the village gets drunk,
Go to the side of the drunks, O Cupbearer.

O Cupbearer,
Whose favor and kindness are expected,
Be quick, offer more and more.
Where is bashfulness? Where is the drunk?
If you are shy, pour one glass
Over the head of shyness.

Get up, O Cupbearer.
Come, O One who is the enemy of bashfulness.
Come to us with a smile,
So our fortune will smile, O Cupbearer.

31.

Every moment, a revelation
Comes to Hearts from the sky.
"How long you do you intend
To stay on earth like sediment?
Ascend to the sky."

Only heavy Souls
Drop to the bottom like sediment.
Once they are purified,
They go to the top.

Don't stir up the mud all the time.
Let turbid water stay still to cleanse itself.
Your dregs can become clean.
The remedy can be found in your grief.

There is a Soul like lightning,
But it is smoke more than light.
When smoke exceeds the limit,
One cannot see the houses' lights.

If you get rid of the smoke,
You'll be enlightened with glory,
Illuminate this and the other world
With your light.

You don't see the moon or sky on muddy water.
The sun and moon are hidden
When the air gets dark.

The South wind cleans the air.
The breeze of early dawn
Can light up the world.

Every breath we take
Cleanses the grief and discomfort in the Soul,
Shines inside of man.
When a man stops breathing one moment,
Nothingness touches his being.

Our bizarre Soul longs
For the land of Nothingness.
Yet I don't know why
The animal self is out to pasture.

O Soul, whose essence is clear and clean,
How long will you wander, take journeys?
You are the falcon of the King.
Fly to the whistle of your King.

An illuminated page from *Bahr-i Recez,*
Dîvân-i Kebîr (c.1368) registered at the
Mevlânâ Museum in Konya.

The Farsi version of Gazel 32 (shown opposite in English), which is one of the three Tercî-Bends of *Bahr-i Recez, Dîvân-i Kebîr* (c.1368), registered at the Mevlânâ Museum in Konya, Turkey. Tercî-Bend is a longer form of lyric poetry than the gazel. In this form, a transition stanza is used to clearly mark the segue from one idea to the next. The other two Tercî-Bends are numbered 112 and 141.

32.

*Y*our face is pleasant, Your disposition good.
The curl of Your hair's sidelock,
Your head, Your face are beautiful.
Your grace, Your manner, Your fruit
Are all pleasant.
Your kindness is as good as your cruelty.

O the appearance of eternal Love,
O His beauty beyond the extreme,
O His face more beautiful than the moon,
O His stature resembles the cypress.
O the most beautiful One adds Soul to Soul,
Gives joy to the Heart.

O the Soul of garden, meadows and jasmine,
O the light of earth and sky,
O the One who comes to help Lovers,
O the peerless cavalry of the square of Hel-etâ.[71]

O the One who sets the table of favors,
O the One who is kind to the bad and greedy,
The parrot is praising You.
So are the partridge and dove.

O eyes of the Chinese beauties,
O Beauty who never frowns,
Never puts on a sour face,
Don't leave the poor.
Don't scratch the face of contention
With your fingers.

O Beauty who makes sultans
Slave-servants to Him,
Even sultans are poor in front of You.
They put their heads down in Your temple
And praise You, searching for words to praise You,
O Sultan who deserves to be praised.

O the One who gives patience to the devout
And belief to the worshipers,
O the One who becomes
A rose garden to the wise,
When they reach union,
Heart's spaciousness becomes vast.

I am with Lovers.
I don't want to sleep tonight.
I will pray for You, O Beloved, until dawn.

I have friends outside
And workers inside of my Heart,
A bunch of charming brothers at home.
They are clean and pure
On the table of Ihvân-i Sefâ.[72]

O the light of gardens and greenery,
O the Cupbearer of cypress and jasmine,
When I mention You, my mouth is sweetened.
I will tell Tercî.

****

You are about to go on a trip alone,
Either to the drunks or to the Beloved,
Swaying from side to side.

I become like a ball, headless and footless,
In front of the club of destiny.
If you are going to the square,
Take me with You. Take me back to my essence.

You are so bright that You fault the sunshine.
The moon looks dark because of You.
If You run around, even the sky will be too small.

You are such an unprecedented Beloved.
You are such a peerless Beauty.
You came so late with so much difficulty,
But you are going so quickly and easily.

O Beautiful, with His face like the sun,
O Jesus, looking for ills,
How fortunate is the crowd
To whom You are going.

Either You are entirely Soul,
Or Hizir[73] of the present, or the Fountain of Life.
That's why You're hidden from the people.

O the Kible[74] of thoughts,
O God's lion in the middle of the forest,[75]
O guide of talents,
You keep walking in the Soul like a mind.

When You take the road of separation,
Lovers lose the glass of mind and intelligence.
Please tear the curtain of shame and modesty
That makes the mistake of calling Soul *mind*.

Never mind separation.
Wherever You go to look for something,
A bright moon with cloudy wet eyes follows You.

O the light of every eye, every mind,
O the One who is brighter than the moon or sun,
Look at the third Tercî.
Look at it carefully.

****

O light inside of the light,
I will ask you a question.
What spell do You cast
That grief becomes joy?

Such sweet lips You have to cast a spell,
Like the Prophet David.
You also soften iron,
Melt and cast different shapes.[76]

No. You may be a Sultan who refuses
To be limited by any restrictions.
You may be the governor of the land of God,
Or the private pupil of the Creator
Who gave up all spells.

I have ridden so many stately horses
Since I have known You.
At last, I threw myself out of trouble.
I am free from fear,
Have reached the land of security.

I am a new Soul in every moment.
I go to a different garden every time.
If You put Your hand on me,
Neither my hand nor my Heart will remain.

****

I know neither the sky nor the star of Süha.[77]
I know neither the garment nor its price.
I know nothing.
All I know is, O my One as beautiful as the moon,
You are my peace and comfort.

O One who gives sustenance
To angels, to people,
O the pivot of this thoughtful sky,
With all these beauties,
Will You forget this guest in Your Heart?
That's impossible.

What a wonderful moment it is
That my cypress-statured Beauty
Grows in the green
And I stand in front of Him,
Trembling like a willow tree in the wind.

The tulip would be washed with blood.
Narcissus would keep looking with jealousy.
The bud would throw its hat from its head.
The iris would pass out from being iris.

O Cupbearer of the assembly of all kindness,
I am Your drunk, Your ruined one.
O rose garden, O garden of Eden,
I am Your guest today.

✿✿✿✿✿✿✿✿✿

Look at those playful eyes
Coming drunk from the tavern.
He tucked His shirt in His belt
To shed the blood of Lovers.

The Beauty of Beauties took an oath:
"I will offer this wine constantly.
Not father, not mother, not anyone
Will remain sober."

"I'll serve so much of this wine,
I'll play such a game with this wine," He said,
"I'll make you all crazy.
In the end, you won't find one sane person
In the world of humans."

Our Leylâ,[78] Cupbearer of Soul,
All the world is her Mecnun.
Everything else is useless, worthless
Besides Leylâ and Mecnun.

Either He takes our stage horse from us
And makes it gallop,
Or pillages everything we have.
Neither ordinary places
Nor places of worship are safe.
How can you be safe from our Love?
Is that possible?

If I don't see you drunk,
I'll throw all your belongings in the fire.
I'll yell and scream.
I'll force you to drink.
I'll make you drunk.

The time for the wise is gone.
This is the time for the Cupbearer.
Give a big glass to the one who denies that.

Winter is gone. Spring is here.
That's the moment the wine meets the glass.
Drink. Listen to the reed.
The time for eating is gone.

That deceitful old woman has left.
So has the winter, rain and mud.
Spring has arrived.
Hundreds of beauties
And hundreds of sweethearts are born.

O Cupbearer, now serve that red wine.
Serve it so the ears will be opened,
And I will tell one more Tercî.

✻✻✻✻✻✻✻✻✻

Threaten as harshly as possible.
Fight as viciously as you can.
Know this:
The smoke coming
From the stokehole of a bath
Doesn't rise very high in the sky.

Even if it does,
It cannot cover the sky.
Even with that, the sky acquires
All its purity and light from the smoke.

O brother, don't hurt yourself.
Don't hit your head against the stones.
You cannot fight with that burned, flamed self.

If you spit at the moon,
Your saliva will land on your face.
If you pull on His shirt,
Your dress gets shorter.

Lots of immature ones before you have also
Boiled, overflowed, fought and struggled
In the kettle of this world.
But they all gave up at the end,
Finding nothing but contention.

One porcupine grabbed the tail of a snake
And pulled its head inside,
Then became like a ball.

That stupid snake started throwing itself
From one spike to another
And became riddled with holes.

That impatient, ugly face,
Without knowing the game,
Killed itself.
If it had waited awhile,
It might have been saved.

You also put yourself together.
Don't throw yourself on the spikes
Of every porcupine of trouble.
Relax when you have accidents.
Say to yourself, "Even the airspace will shrink."

The Creator of all universes said,
"I am with the One who has patience."
O the One who stays with patience,
Pour patience on our head.
Give us patience.

I've gone to another valley.
You tell the rest of it.
Give our greetings to the patient One
Again and again.

33.

Put Your mind in Your head,
O Doctor of Love.
Have you ever seen any Lover like us?
O Beloved, I would be long gone without You.

O Joseph, of all the hundreds gathering,
Have you ever seen a Jacob like me
Who has been engulfed by grief?
My face turned a pale yellow
Because of the grief of Love.
My eyes became blind from crying.

O Joseph, look at me and see the tears
Coming from the eyes of poor Jacob.
Because of Love,
Tears keep coming from my eyes.

There are hundreds of Egypts,
Hundreds of reed beds in the Heart of Joseph.
"Either small or big,
Game is in the stomach of wild donkeys."[79]

The chance for drink, joy and pleasure
Have all gotten better.
Whatever my Heart has desired has happened.
But rest assured, "Time is a sharp sword." [80]
Don't think of the past.

For Love, play with your Soul.
Don't say, like the Israelites said to Moses,
"You and your God go and fight.
We'll stay here."[81]

You cannot find milder people
Than these Lovers of this world.
Tell the wise and intelligent people,
"Be kind to Lovers."

If you have fallen into grief,
In the end, with the favor of God,
Whose compassion and justice cover the arch,
You will be helped and relieved.[82]

If you know us, if you are familiar
With our beautiful, graceful Cupbearer,
Grab Him. Don't let Him go.
Nobody else has anything for you.

O One who teaches tricks to the wise,
We have tried all the tricks and deceits,
But You are the One
Who sees and does everything,
The One who sees and knows the unseen.

Be silent! Listen to the rest of it
From the One whose disposition is kindness.
As a matter of fact,
Understanding is given
As a remedy for every bad thing
Because of His favor.

34.

That hodja [83] became ill suddenly
In the middle of the night.
He had lost himself
And kept hitting his head against the wall
Until morning.

The sky and earth cried and yelled for him.
He looked like he had fallen into fire.
Even his breath was burning.

He had a bizarre sickness.
He didn't have a headache.
He didn't have malaria.
There is no cure in this world for this disease,
Because it came from the sky.

Galinos [84] came and examined his pulse.
He said, "Leave my hand alone.
Look at my Heart.
My disease is not in the books."

There was much talk and discussion in our city:
"What kind of disease is that?
He has no bile, no passion,
No muscle aches, no edema.

"He doesn't sleep, doesn't talk.
He is fed by Love.
Love is like a nanny, like a mother to him."

"O my God," I said. "Help him
So he can rest for a moment.
He hasn't hurt anyone.
He hasn't stolen anything."

A voice came from the sky.
"Leave him alone
Because there is no medicine
For the illness of Lovers.

"Don't bother this hodja.
Don't tie him up. Don't advise him.
The place he has fallen into
Is neither the place of worship
Nor the place of bad things."

What do you think about Love?
You haven't heard about Love, even from Lovers.
Be silent. Don't try to cast a spell.
Love is neither a tale nor a game.

O Shems of Tebriz, come,
O Source of mine, O Source of light!
This great stately Soul
Is dull and lifeless without Your light.

35.

Be lost in grief, O Soul.
Patience is the key to suffering.
Be lost in grief
That in the end He will show His face.
Patience is the key to suffering. [85]

Plunge into pain and suffering
So deeply that at the bottom,
The Throne of God[86] comes suddenly
To your temple.
Patience is the key to suffering.

Smile with the light of the earth.
Be the wedding feast of the earth.
Leave mourning, reach security,
Because patience is the key to suffering.

O my Heart, give up men and women.
Pull their love out from inside you.
With Love, He becomes
Your paternal and maternal uncle,
Because patience is the key to suffering.

If you bend double like the sky
And go with God's command,
You'll be saved from destiny and its twisted ways.
Patience is the key to suffering.

At the same time, you'll be saved from self,
Grab the hair of the devil and cut his throat.
Patience is the key to suffering.

Your fortune comes to your feet,
Success to your side.
Be honored by His presence.
Patience is the key to suffering.

A trouble bothers you inside;
That's the reason things don't go well for you.
Tie up that trouble neatly.
Patience is the key to suffering.

There is a wonderful world of God.
Don't look for it in this imaginary world
For even one moment.
God is the only confidant
For this world.
Patience is the key to suffering.

Be silent! Don't tell the secret.
Strangers cannot reach the secret of Min ledün.[87]
Patience is the key to suffering.

36.

Rinds[88] are greeting you.
Their Souls become slaves and servants to you.
They become drunk with your cup.
"Drunks are greeting you."

I became the topic of talk for everyone
Because of Your Love,
Which made me meaner.
"Drunks are greeting you."

Look at this divine struggle.
Watch this flood-like torrent.
See this Sun of God.
"Drunks are greeting you."

One is casting spells on me.
One is expecting me to repent.
One keeps running without feet, like me.
"Drunks are greeting you."

O desire of desires, lift this curtain.
I don't know anyone but Him.
"Drunks are greeting you."

O cloud which rains so beautifully!
Come, O drunkenness of friends.
Come, O Sultan who steals the Heart.
"Drunks are greeting you."

Astonish us. Get us out of trouble.
Ruin us, but fill us up with treasures.
Count the eternal money which is in our hand.
"Drunks are greeting you."

The entire town turned upside down for you.
At times, they all have known you.
Other times, they haven't known you at all.
O the One who gives the Heart
The power to see and perceive,
"Drunks are greeting you."

Tell the One whose face
Is more beautiful than the moon,
The One whose eyes are like a magician,
Tell that good-mannered Sultan,
"Drunks are greeting you."

Tell the man of the brawl,
The brave of the war,
That confusion, that Love,
That fresh green cypress,
"Drunks are greeting you."

To the place where no one with right mind exists,
To the place where no one but one drunk fits,
To the land with no road, no religion, no creed!
"Drunks are greeting you."

Tell the Soul who is beyond
The question of what and how,
Tell the sweetheart who trapped Mecnun,
Tell the hidden pearl,
"Drunks are greeting you."

The One who is a trap for the people,
The One who is the Soul of the world,
Tell that Love, that constant companion,
"Drunks are greeting you."

Tell that blue sea,
Tell that watching eye,
Tell Mount Sinai,
"Drunks are greeting you."

Tell the One who broke my repentance,
The One who patches my mantle,
Tell the light of my days,
"Drunks are greeting you."

Tell my Kurban bayram,[89]
Tell that light of the Koran,
Tell the One who is praised
At the door of Heaven,[90]
"Drunks are greeting you."

O our Sultan Husameddin,
O the man whom all saints praise,
O the One with whose help
All become aware of their Soul,
"Drunks are greeting you."

37.

Go tell that Rebab player,
"Drunks are greeting you."
Run tell that moor hen,[91]
"Drunks are greeting you."

Tell that man who is serving drinks,
"Drunks are greeting you."
Tell that permanent life,
"Drunks are greeting you."

Tell the man of this tumult,
"Drunks are greeting you."
Tell that confusion, that Love,
"Drunks are greeting you."

O most Beautiful
Whose face makes the moon ashamed,
"Drunks are greeting you."
O peace and comfort of the Heart,
"Drunks are greeting you."

O the One who is the Soul of Soul,
"Drunks are greeting you."
O that much Beauty and beyond,
"Drunks are greeting you."

There is nobody by himself there.
Here, there is nobody but one who is drunk.
"Drunks are greeting you."

O wish of wishes,
"Drunks are greeting you."
Lift the veil off of your face.
"Drunks are greeting you."

38.

No one's advice will ever help Lovers.
Love is such a torrent
That no one can stand in front of it.

The mind will never understand
The pleasure of the drunk.
The wise will never know
The value of the dirt in front of the door
Of the One who has gone beyond himself.

Kings would give away their throne
For the smell of the wine that Lovers drink
At the assembly of Heart.

Husrev[92] left his kingdom for Shirin.
Ferhad[93] tried to make a tunnel in the mountain
For the same reason.

Mecnun[94] stays out of normal people's circle
Because of his love for Leylâ.
Vamik[95] keeps smiling
At the beard and mustache of the unruly ones
Because of Love.

O my Beauty,
Without the awareness of Soul,
Life is frozen.
The One who doesn't know the pass
Finds the abyss on the road.
Without news from the Beloved,
His brain is decayed.

If this sky weren't in Love like us,
If this sky's head weren't as dizzy as ours,
It would give up this whirling
And say, "Enough!"
How long would I whirl? How long?

The whole universe is like a reed flute.
He keeps blowing from every hole.
Every cry knows the pleasure
Of those two sweet lips.

Look and see. Every time He blows
On a bit of earth, on every Heart,
He gives them a need, offers a Love,
And they cry with grief
Because of that sorrow.

If you take God out of your Heart,
With whom are you going to be in Love?
Tell me.
The one who takes Him out of his Heart
For even one moment
Is lifeless.

I'll be silent. You go quickly
And climb up on the roof at night.
O Soul, send an uproar to the town.

39.

Verse 546

Today, we are smiling and happy
Because that good fortune is coming.
Our beautiful Sultan of Sultans is coming.

Today I will break my vow.
I'll throw away my diet,
Because the Beauty of Joseph
Is coming from the land of Canaan.

I go swaying like a drunk.
I go secretly like a Soul
In the direction of that Sultan,
Searching, asking along the way.

The stately palace is built.
The sky has untied its turban
And is walking with great difficulty,
Because it's coming
From the assembly of the drunks.

O son, follow our orders.
Be faithful to us, O son.
Don't go buy on terms, O son.
Look. Orders are coming today.

Be enlightened like the sky.
Blossom like the rose garden.
Try to swim like a fish.
That endless sea is coming.

Come to your senses, O son.
Come to your senses.
Don't look at me. Look at yourself,
Because the smell of saffron[97]
Makes the one who talks laugh.

You came back again, clapping your hands.
You'll ruin the houses again,
Because the bright sun
Is coming to the run-down places.

O the one who's stayed at home,
You've grown in the shade.
Go outside,
Because the Sun turns ordinary stone
Into the Ruby of Bedehsan.[98]

Sometimes He is bloody.
Other times He drinks blood.
Sometimes He takes care of the ill
And cures them,
Especially this hopeless one,
Because he came from their side.

Look for the drunks today.
See my secret things.
Don't see or talk about my shames.
I am so drunk because of Him
That words are coming from my mouth
And falling all over the place in utter confusion.

40.

The Soul who is not in Love with the faithful
Is so disloyal.
God will curse the one
Who is not in Love with the Grace of God.

O Sultan who deserves the words:
"His eyes haven't moved
From what he has seen! "[99]
He has visited all around the world,
Has seen a figure,
But he wasn't in Love with figures.

I heard this yesterday from a bunch of fairies.
They gathered at the door of the town.
They said, "Give a house in the village
To the one who doesn't like our city."

Pity the fish
That falls on dry soil.
Pity the copper
That hasn't been in Love with chemistry.

Where is the Soul that hasn't tried
To merge with his origin?
Why won't iron fall in Love
With the magnet?

The door of death is closed to him.
He can't escape soon.
He doesn't deserve to live,
Yet he isn't in Love with death.

41.

Who is the One who gives grief to the Heart,
But when you cry at His temple,
Your grief is sweetened?

At first, He appears to be a snake.
In the end, He becomes a treasure, a pearl.
He is such a Sultan
That He turns suffering into sweet pleasure.

He makes the devil
Into the most beautiful girl in heaven
And changes mourning into a wedding party.
He makes a wise man out of one born blind.

He enlightens the dark
And turns the thorn into a rose garden.
He pulls the sliver out of your palm
And makes a cushion out of rose petals.

He gives fire to His Abraham,
But He transforms the fire of Nimrod[100]
Into the roses of August.

He is the One who gives light to the stars.
He is the One who helps the needy.
He does favors for His creatures,
Then He gives praise to them.

He drops the guilt of the guilty,
Like autumn leaves,
And suggests words of apology
To the ear of the one
Who says bad things about Him.

He says, "O loyal man,
Ask for forgiveness for your guilt."
When the man starts praying,
He secretly says, "Amen."

Because He knows the Amen
Of the one to whom
He gives the pleasure of praying,
After prayers, He turns that person
Inside out like a fig, sweet and beautiful.

He gives power to hands and feet
In good work and bad,
In such pleasure that the body assumes
The strains of Rüstem.[101]

With enjoyment, the lean man becomes Rüstem.
Without it, Rüstem falls into pain and suffering.
If this pleasure is not
The companion of the Soul,
The Soul won't have peace and quietness.

I sent the Soul to Tebriz in early dawn
To praise Shemseddin.
He knows the way to go.

42.

Verse 575

The spring of the Lovers has come
To make the earth a garden and meadow.
A voice is heard from the sky
For the bird of Soul to fly.

The sea is filled with pearls.
At the same time, bitter water
Becomes a river of Kevser.[102]
Stone turns to ruby in the mine.
At the same time, the body becomes Soul.

The Soul's eyes of Lovers
Rain a flood like clouds,
But their hearts shine
Like lightning in God's clouds.

Do you know why the eyes of Lovers
Turned into clouds with Love?
Because that moon was hidden in the clouds.

What a happy, joyful moment it is
When those clouds cry.
My God, what an auspicious moment it is
When those lightnings laugh.

There is not even one drop
That comes to earth
Out of those hundreds of thousands of drops.
If one did,
It would destroy the whole world.

The whole world would be ruined by Love.
So many would board Noah's ark,
So many turn to be confident
And not worry about the flood.

If the flood calms down, the sky won't turn.
That wave can't fit any dimension.
Because the six dimensions keep moving.

O the One who is bound with six dimensions,
Be oppressed by sorrow or not.
At the same time, those seeds
Will shove up from the ground,
Grow and become date palms.

There will be a day
When that root raises its head above the ground
And becomes a new branch.
Even if a few of the branches become dry,
The rest of them will bud and grow.

Those dried branches burn and become fire.
This fire is good for the people, like Soul.
If this is not the case,
Then the opposite is:
One either becomes green or becomes fire.

Something is closing my mouth.
I am at the edge of the roof,
At the same time, I am drunk.
The thing which admires you
Is also admired by Him.

43.

The sun went to sleep. Time is gone.
It's night now.
The sun has descended into the well.
The sun of the Lover's Soul
Has gone to God's privacy.

A Turk among Indians
Is like a day in the night.
Don't make noise at night
Because that Turk has gone to his tent now.

If you get a smell from this brightness,
You set your sleep on fire, burn it.
Even Venus becomes a friend of the moon
By walking and serving at night.

We're running away at night.
The Indians are pursuing us,
Because we've stolen gold,
And the doorkeeper has gotten the news.

We've learned how to walk in the night,
How to get rid of hundreds of doorkeepers.
Our cheeks blaze and glitter like candles
And make kings out of our pawns.

What glory to that face
That rubs His face.
What greatness to that Heart
That is turned into the abode
Of all Heart's desire.

Who hasn't sighed on the way to Heart?
It's good for the one
Who has plunged into the waters of this sigh.

If he sinks into the sea,
The sea carries him to its head,
Like Joseph who fell in the well
And then reached glory.

It is said that man comes from earth
And eventually returns there.
Why would the one who is the earth of this door
Become earth?
Is it possible?

Crops are all alike until harvest.
But at the threshing,
Half becomes grain, the other straw.

44.

𝒥t's too late, too late.
The sun has gone down the well.
But O good fortune, Beauty,
It's time for the moon to rise again.

Cupbearer, walk toward the glass.
Doorkeeper, climb to the roof.
O restless, uneasy Soul,
Go. That Sultan wants privacy.

The tears which enlightened the eyes,
The patience which burned my harvest to ashes,
Even the mind
To whom you teach the rules of the game,
They've all left.
They disappeared in the middle of the night.

O men whose bright eyes enlightened the night
With their glory!
The night that resembles an Indian[103]
Has escaped screaming,
Yelling, "That Turk is coming into the tent!"

With good moves,
The pawn will be gone, and Vizier will come.
With the help of that auspicious Beauty,
The Vizier is gone, and the Shah has come.

At night, Souls reach their proper places,
And intentions are realized.
The One who understands and appreciates this
Will acquire a Soul as bright as day.

O day, are you the Last Day of Judgement?
O night, are you the Night of Kadir?[104]
Or the tree in which God manifested to Moses?

The moon threshes the stars at night.
O day, go away.
The Milky Way is filled with straw,
Because that galaxy entered the sign of Virgo,
Its face covered with straw.

Don't be heedless at the well of the flesh.
Grab the bucket of sky.
Joseph got out of the well
Because he held that bucket,
Freed himself from the well,
Reached glory.

Look for purification in the dark night,
Like Muhammad.
That Sultan ascended in one night
And became a unique, peerless One.

The whole universe becomes silent
Because of the night.
Start searching and carrying on wholeheartedly.
The peace at the land of privacy
Is disturbed because of noises.

O Shems of Tebriz,
You don't need the cover of night.
You've slipped out of it.
You don't belong to the East and West.
Now the words have ceased.

45.

𝔍t's late night now.
The sun has descended into the well.
The sun of the Souls of Lovers
Has gone to God's privacy.

A Turk among the Indians
Is like a day in the night.
Be quiet at night,
Because that Turk has already gone to his tent.

If you get the smell of this daylight,
You burn the night.
Venus became the peer of the moon
By walking and serving at night.

We're running away at night.
The Indians are after us,
Because we've stolen gold.
The watchman knows that.

We've learned to walk at night.
We got rid of, burned, hundreds of watchmen.
Our cheeks shine like the moon
Because our pawns became Shahs.

The bazaar of the earth is all gone.
Watch the bazaar of the stars.
Dawn is becoming like a bazaar,
Full of stars and priceless pearls.

How long will I be suffering
From this body's horse?
It keeps asking constantly for straw and barley.
Yet in the sky, the galaxy of the Milky Way
Is full of straw for him.

The saddle horse doesn't have
A share of this glory.
That peerless Soul is the One
Who has a share of that Kingdom.

You've seen the body,
Now look at the Soul.
You've seen the jewel,
Now look at the mine.
Look at the peerless, strange fate that,
Once it gets into Him,
Loses its way.

Meaning constantly says,
"Don't dress me in these old clothes."
Words are really old shirts,
Such old shirts that everyone makes fun of them.

I say, "O meaning, come.
Get in a form like the Soul
So that old shirts and clothes
Become silk with Soul's light."

Quit washing clothes
So that the fairies won't hear.[105]
Never mind the fairies.
That Soul is tired.
Even from the angels who are close to God,
He wants privacy.

46.

Verse 621

Since I have seen Your glory,
The world has fallen into disesteem in my eyes.
And given up the surmise of existence.

Lightning has flashed from the place
That has no beginning of the beginning.
The whole universe has burned to ashes.
When the glory of union opened the flag,
All I's and we's fell to pieces.

We're separated from the motherland;
That's why we're tired and in trials.
How can one be confident
When he's away from his country?

The Cupbearer grabbed a glass
Instead of the Koran.
A spark dropped on our shirt
From that hot glass.
We are burning.

47.

Verse 625

A vain man came to the garden of Soul
To eat melon.
Have you ever seen a donkey
Eat goat meat in this world?

The wise and brave eat the early melon
Grown at the garden of Soul,
Not the oxen or donkeys.

Food for the one who lives in the West
Comes from Spain.
The one who lives in the East
Is nourished with food from Hurmuz.[106]

The one who serves the Kaiser
Gets food from the Kaiser.
If he is the servant of Urbuz,[107]
He is fed by Urbuz's kitchen.

The one who steals and bullies
Is eventually handled by law officers
And subject to the torture of Oguz.[108]

The one called Turk is such
That the village is sure to pay taxes
Because they're afraid of him.
Not so for the one
Who is hit and slapped by everyone
Because of his greed.

The smart person doesn't worry
About not having beaver fur in springtime.
He doesn't bother with furs then.

The one who has excess bile
Doesn't like sweet pomegranates
Because of his bad character.
He likes bitter ones.
That's good for him.

Be silent! The one who has
The appetite of an ox
And eats the beans and grapes of ten people
Is unable to drink the Soul's wine.

48.

*Y*our Love flows like the Fountain of Life
In the canal of Soul.
Even the Fountain of Life
Runs with Your Love in the canal,
Searching for You.

The world is full of the melodies of birds
Which are praising You.
The bird of my Heart flies away
Once birds are mentioned.

I give my Soul with pleasure
When I hear these melodies.
Why shouldn't the Soul smile
While leaving the flesh,
Remembering the Beloved?

Every bird of Soul makes circles.
Each one of them has his own cage.
Each one is like me,
Going toward the temple of Solomon.

There is every moment a spiritual ecstasy
From the Soul of the Ones
Who go to the Throne of God drunk,
Without existence.

What is Soul?
The jar of great Sultans.
There is wine of sky inside.
Because of that,
The words are going, scattered like Lovers.

There is another pleasure
In my eating, my living.
There is another pleasure
In my talking.
The rest of them go like that.

In the meantime,
We've been playing with You at this place.
O most Beautiful, what a nice place!
But this is not a square for those
Whose horse is limping;
They all leave this place.

The moon has put itself like a ball
In front of Your club.
The sun is playing with its Soul,
Rolling like a ball.

The moon and sun are always running,
But they haven't found the way to Your temple.
They're just covered by Your halo.
They walk out of the tent.

If the brilliance outside is like that,
O my God,
How could the One who reaches Your glory
Be sober?
He shines and shines, O my God.

49.

Don't think of profit and self-interest.
Those are the signs of poverty.
Clean people make contributions.
They get into God's habit.

With Love, in the end,
There will be no greed and no generosity.
Some hidden return is expected
In every generosity.

Generosity is like taking a journey.
Greed is like standing still.
But if you've boarded Noah's Ark,
Journeys and stations are not important.

All those forms and names
Which have piled up in hundreds of layers
Will lose their quality and quantity
At the sea of glory which covers every where,
The sea where everything turns to Him
And becomes Him.

O poor shepherd, Love is the staff of Moses
In this world of existence.
In real existence, in front of Him,
His manifestations and appearances
Are nothing but forms created by a magician.

Escape from drowning
In front of the whirlpool of flesh.
Existence and joy all come
From that world which gives light
To this six dimensional world.

Shake yourself off like a tree.
Shake off green leaves as well as dry ones.
Once the colors of goodness and badness
Disappear,
Union and Oneness appear.

Go on your way.
Don't ask what or why,
Because He is beyond quality and quantity.
You are a gazelle.
What are you doing with lions?

Be silent. Words are the sign of separation.
When a brave man is chewing bread,
How can he ask for more bread?

50.

Why has the Sufi sobered?
Why has the Cupbearer stopped serving?
If one drunkenness goes to sleep,
Another drunkenness is awakened.

When the sun goes down,
The world is illuminated by You.
When Your beautiful eyes become languid,
Earth squeezes its eyes.

If the first drink dries up,
There are hundreds of new ones.
Since Your hair became a chain,
We've become crazy.

O beautifully-voiced singer,
Watch the first and last drinking.
Now no one listens to the other's spell,
Because everyone has learned the secret.

My Sultan, we are Moses.
You are sometimes a staff, sometimes a dragon.
O beautiful ones, your prices come down
Because it is the time
When Bulgars[109] come looting.

Your ruby lips have sucked the sugar cane.
Your eyes are ruined with envy.
The Soul has cleaned and prepared
The house of the Heart.
Come back to yourself.
It is time for Union.

You give excuses all the time,
Avoiding and running away from me.
O Soul, why are you ignoring me?
Isn't it enough yet?

O stone-hearted Beauty,
No excuses tonight.
You are the moon, we are a star.
Tonight the moon will meet the star.

O the moon cannot fit into the dawn.
Tonight we are Your guest.
Once the night covers the world with curtains,
It's time for people to walk alone.

I have suffered from your pain and troubles.
You thought I was dead.
No, you are pure and clean.
I am sediment.
Nowadays drinks are not pure and clean.
They are drinking sediment.

With Your Union-like mornings,
With Your separation that burns the worlds,
With Your Love that teaches deceit,
So many naive ones have become deceitful.

I didn't have a fever.
I didn't have a heartache.
Yet I knocked my head on the wall until morning.
I became ill because of the desire
For rose marmalade.

51.

We don't do anything
But serve our Cupbearer.
The Cupbearer offers more cups
So that I will be saved from good and bad.

God created everyone for one job.
He created us for the art of joblessness.

Every day we keep playing
In front of this light, like particles.
Every night we turn like stars
Around the Beloved
Whose face is like the moon.

If You expected work from us,
You wouldn't offer this wine.
The one who drinks this wine
Doesn't bend his head down to earth.

What kind of job can a drunk do?
A drunk does whatever the wine wants.
God's wine would destroy both worlds
Until man reaches God,
Who doesn't need anything.

You'll wake up from the drunkenness of this world
After a good night's sleep.
But the drunkenness from God's wine
Will last until the grave.

O neighbors, free wine comes from Grace.
Those Cupbearers
Are kind, protective and sweet to the child,
Like nannies.

Heart, get drunk beyond the limit.
Wherever you go, go drunk.
Makes others drunk, too,
So that He will offer you one more cup.

Wherever you see a Beauty,
Sit in front of her like a mirror.
As for the ugly, cover the mirror with carpet.

Play with the Beautifuls around town.
Say secretly, "I make an oath to this town." [110]
What holy, happy town is that?

My head is dizzy from this wine.
I've become drunk.
It's time to be quiet, engulfed in silence.
It's impossible to count
All the favors and kindnesses
That I have received.

52.

When the Lover breathes,
Flames spread through the universe.
One breath shatters this illusionary world
Into particles.

The world becomes an ocean
From beginning to end,
And the ocean disappears in its majesty.
If this were made manifest for even a second
To the people,
There would be no humanity left.

Smoke rises to the sky, so thick
That no human, no angel can exist there.
Suddenly a fire comes out of this smoke
And covers the whole sky.

The sky splits at that moment.
Time, space and existence all disappear.
An uproar fills the world,
A wedding joy descends after the mourning.

Sometimes He puts fire into water.
Sometimes water extinguishes the fire.
Sometimes He blows a wind
To send the waves of the sea of Absence
To the eighth level of the Atlas sky.

Even the sun loses its light
Because of the brilliance of a human's Soul.
Don't ask anything from the people
When even the confident talk little of the secret.

In front of this secret,
Mars loses it masculinity;
Jupiter burns its book;
The moon's greatness disappears,
Its joy turned into grief.

Mercury becomes stuck in mud;
Saturn burns with fire;
Venus loses its posture
And starts striking tunes of joy.

There will be neither rain nor rainbow,
Neither wine nor glass,
No drink, no cheer, no salve for the wound.

Water doesn't form designs;
Wind doesn't cover the ground;
The garden doesn't become beautiful;
And April's rain doesn't kiss the earth.

Neither illness nor remedy stays,
Neither friend nor enemy.
There is neither reed flute nor melody;
Neither a high-pitched tune
Nor a low one is played.

Causes stay behind.
The Cupbearer gives wine to himself.
Soul says, "God is great."
Heart says, "God knows better."

Get up. Look.
The painter of eternity has started to work again,
To design unmatched figures
On the clothes of the creatures He desires.

God started a fire to burn all untrue things.
Fire burns the Heart
And takes him to the middle of that universe.

God is sun. Heart is dawn's sky,
Such a dawn that every ray of light
Reflects on Edhemogul[111]
And Jesus, son of Mary.

53.

Once the fire of the Heart blazes,
It burns the faithful as well as the unfaithful.
Once the bird of essence flies,
All of existence disappears.

The world is demolished.
The Soul plunges into flood.
The same water which melts pearl into water
Creates pearl again.

Hidden secrets become obvious.
The forms of earth are broken down.
Suddenly a gigantic wave
Comes and rises to the emerald sky.

At times it becomes paper and pen.
At times, he passes out.
The Soul becomes an enemy to good and bad
And keeps wounding them every moment.

The Soul who reaches God
Enters the privacy of the Sultan.
If it was a snake, then it became a fish,
Escaped from the ground and plunged into the sea
To merge with the River of Kevser.[112]

While in space,
He reaches the world of Absence.
He appears in that universe.
Wherever he is dropped afterwards,
He smells musk and turns it into ambergris.

He is in poverty in Absence,
But He is a guide to the stars.
He becomes dust at the door of Hakan,[113]
Then knocks at the door of Sencer.[114]

A voice comes to the Heart from flame,
Flame that burns the sun:
"Leave this light alone
So the light of your Soul
Will be awakened and illuminate the universe."

You serve the Beloved.
Why are you hiding yourself?
O gold, after being hammered
By that goldsmith's hand,
Say, "This is better. It is better this way."

The Heart which is drunk
From the wine of eternity
Passes himself through the telling of this gazel.
If he held his breath and remained silent,
He would do even better.

54.

Drunkenness is sending its greetings,
Giving information secretly to You.
The one whose Heart You grabbed
Makes his Soul a slave to You.

O One who turns existence
Into non-existence,
Receive the greeting of the drunk.
He is so drunk
That he keeps catching his hands and feet
In Your trap.

O sky of Lovers,
The one who becomes Soul to the Soul of Lovers,
Your beauty offers wine among the Lovers,
Saying cheers to your Love.
Your Love made you pray
For the goodness of Lovers.

O the One who is the taste of every lip,
The Kible[115] of every creed,
Moon is turning around Your house every night,
Guarding You.

O Heart, what kind of drunk are You?
How nice are You?
You turned into a Sultan.
You are the Sultan.
With all this greatness,
How does Love subjugate you to Himself?

The One who pulls his Heart out of this earth,
Whose fortune goes to the star of Saturn,
O flesh made from dirt,
O smoke which comes from the fire of Heart,
See what shape He puts you in
If you stay on the ground or fly to the sky.

Take the glass from the hand
Of the Sultan's Cupbearer.
Be drunk like the One who has reached eternity.
If you are half drunk,
You haven't been completed yet.
You are deficient.
He wants to make you totally drunk.

O unique, peerless person,
Your greeting comes like lightning from Your lips.
This greeting cannot be contained
By the lips of the mouth.
The One who attains Your greeting
Gives You the whole favor.

The moon has been split in two with your grief.
Faces have turned silverish.
They look very pale and straight.
A stature like *elif*[116] has become *cim*[117]
That *cim* shapes you like a *cam*.[118]

Hear all those yells and screams
That are caused by Love.
Look at all the tears.
Watch all the things that the jar does,
How it cooks the rawness and matures you.

Look at the wine.
Its color and bouquet are so beautiful.
With His generous hands,
Look how nicely He gives You to the Soul,
But denies the body.

I should be Soul instead of body.
I should be the source instead of the pearl.
O Heart, don't be afraid of having a bad name.
He is giving you a good name.

Enough! Quit talking back and forth.
Don't say any more poems or prose,
Because this deceitful Beauty
Has started talking with you.

55.

Drunkenness is sending its greeting to you.
Is sending news to you secretly.
The one whose Heart You grabbed
Makes his Soul a slave to You.

O the One who makes existence non-existent,
Hear the greeting of the drunk.
He is so drunk
That he keeps catching his hands and feet
In Your trap.

O sky of Lovers,
Your beauty, which is Soul to Lover's Soul,
Offers wine and cheers to Your Love,
And asks you to pray
For the goodness of Lovers.

O the One who is the taste of every lip,
The Kible[119] of every creed,
The moon is turning around Your house
Every night, guarding You.

O the One who makes a body out of earth
And changes smoke into the stars of Saturn!
What a shape it makes
Out of your earthen body, your smoky Soul!

Sometimes He gives you wings and you fly.
Other times, He gives you iron
And you anchor like a ship.
One moment, He makes you morning.
Another, He makes you evening.

One moment He makes you tremble.
Another moment, He makes you laugh.
One moment He makes you drunk
The next, He turns you into a wine glass.

You are like Muhre[120]in His hand.
Sometimes you are wine.
Sometimes you are drunk because of Him.
But once He breaks this Muhre,
I swear by God, He makes you wholly mature.

Sometimes this, sometimes that,
But your end is to realize the truth.
Putting you through this color or that one
Is maturing you, subjugating you.

You were like Noah once
And went through lots of trouble.
You endured.
Now He makes you sail like a ship
Without feet, without steps.

Be silent. Sit with astonishment.
Be astonished by astonishing.
You are a man with wise words,
But words sometimes get out of condition.

56.

Again, another sour-faced someone dropped in.
He's like cold winter.
O sugar-like, sweet Cupbearer,
Pour a glass of wine on his head.

Either give him wine or get rid of him,
Because it's not proper to have a devil
Among the rose faces, O son.

Give him the wine of the Prophet
So the donkey won't be a donkey anymore.
With the wine of Jesus,
He would grow two wings and fly to the sky.

Don't let any sober ones
Enter the assembly of the Heart's drunk.
As you know,
Drunks can do something good or evil
While they are drunk.

O doorkeeper, sit at the door.
Don't let anyone in
Except the Lover whose mouth smells his lungs,
His Heart full of fire.

Other than this kind of Lover,
If you ask for a hand, he gives you a foot.
If you ask for a foot, he gives you a head.
If you want to borrow a spade,
He gives you an axe.

When I'm covered with blood,
Neither my mind nor my modesty stays with me.
I become a crazy, insane Lover.
I'm not safe or sane.
I'm like a shield in front of the sword.

I'm looking for a singer
To become the living Fountain of Life
And sing sometimes until early dawn,
Throwing sleep to the fire.

If you find that one vessel of my body
Is sober while I am at His door,
If he is not drunk at the square of God,
If he is unable to hunt the lion,
Consider him a dog on this way.

One group of people is ruined, drunk, nice.
The other is the slave of five and six.[121]
One is different than the other.

I've drunk beyond the limit.
I've gone beyond the boundary.
Tie my hands. Close my mouth.
It's necessary to protect the drunk.

Relieve our suffering.
Hear our cry.
Pass us beyond ourselves, just like You.
Watch us in that shape.

57.

O most Beautiful, whose chin is so sweet,
Give us the golden wine
So that our Heart will become enlightened
And our eyes more shiny.

Out of obstinacy to the sober,
Give this big glass.
The body becomes Soul;
Night turns into dawn.

When You make sleep go away, offer God's wine.
It's not Your Grace
To close two doors at the same time.

O one who drinks the wine of benevolence,
Don't blame me for anything,
Because the one who thanks will be saved,
Not the one who denies favor.

O the one who stays at the tavern,
Drunk and ruined,
Even then, O one born bad and no good,
Why are you blaming us?

58.

Really, we opened your eyes.
Try to see the hidden things.
Really, we stand among you
And watch the good news come
From the One who came to help you.

O morning breeze, O One
Who brings good news,
Take my Heart for the good news.
I have a Soul in my hand.
I will gladly sacrifice it for You.

If the swords become armour,
The ruins become rose gardens.
The day becomes shinier
If we have attained Your look.

O grief which doesn't have teeth to bite,
O kindness which smiles
Hundreds of hundreds of times,
Since the Soul has reached victory,
Now the Soul smiles.
The universe smiles.

O greatest of the great,
Whoever has seen You in that greatness
And still talks about skill
Should be ashamed in front of God.

That lion of the forest
Hasn't left one vessel in our existence.
We have only half our mind left,
And that is only to rave about the difference
Between day and night,
To talk about separation.

Praise the beauty of the Sultan.
The moon is ashamed after seeing Him.
The blind one opened his eyes and said,
"Wonderful,"
Over and over again.
Even the deaf heard His favors.

I am like a cloud for Him.
He is my moon.
He is my day. I am His night.
He is my Soul. I am like His body.
I admire His beauty, anyway.

How will my Soul be filled
With the Love of my Sultan?
Why won't I need that medicine, that remedy?
I have an oxen's appetite in my Soul.

Even my joy and pleasure are gone.
My mind is clouded with insomnia.
I swear to God,
My Soul hasn't given Him up,
Hasn't denied His favor.

O from prayer without a hearer,
Guilt without a forgiver,
Disease without a proper doctor or remedy,
My face is so pale, like gold,
Without that silver-statured beauty.

When will it be time
For me to give thanks to God
Because I have obtained my pearl?
When that time comes,
I will lay down with joy under that tree.

When I see my Beloved,
When I look for relief from my grief,
I will tell my story of separation
And then show the blood of my lungs.

O pearl of existence and eternity,
You are concealed like God.
Your face has been hidden.
The Beauty whom everyone serves,
The One who is Master of everyone
Is Shemseddin,
Whose town is Tebriz.
He is known and famous there.

59.

Spring is here.
The time of joy and cheer is here;
Winter has gone.
With the grace of God,
Who pardons all mistakes and sins,
We have passed the dangerous season.

God is revealed to you, saying,
"We forgive your sins.
Don't worry about the things you've lost.
Be content, for contentment is the best virtue."

There are many who say secretly
That we are the only ones who know His favor.
Never mind this.
We know His secret.
Don't pay much attention
To things already seen and heard.

O young man, the secret is in you.
Don't ask for it from a stranger,
From the one who comes and goes.
There is no use in something
Which has already been explored.

Look at all the humiliated people.
Most of them have seen
The light of the right way.
Once the moon is split,
Their curtain won't be raised again.

O our God, O God who has compassion, favor,
If You don't pity us, who will?
To lead us the right or wrong way
Is all under Your power.
The rest is illusion and deception.

O desire, where is purification, realization?
How long will you struggle with the rhyme?
We have clean dispositions;
We eliminate grief and anxiety.

If my words are scattered,
My Love, the One who protects and watches me,
Has grown, spread.
Love is a long, very long time for us,
And the great Sultan is among us.

This is such a secret
That it's hard to talk about.
It is such a sword
That it gleams too much.
The sun cannot be hidden in the early morning
Unless a sorcerer puts a spell on it.

O magician who closes our eyes,
You've already put us under Your spell.
Comfort us now,
Or accept the place where we choose to live.
That is the place of insomnia.

O people of Moses,
We are also lost in the desert.
How did you find the way out?
Tell us. Don't hide this from us.

It didn't matter
If water took away our food and belongings.
Food rained on us from the sky.[122]
God put us in an orderly way.
Now it is a pleasure to travel
Or to make a stop on the journey.

Love cheated us after it made us happy.
You repair the damage with Your kindness.
The Prophet said, "Produce no harm."[123]

We will consider what we'll do about you.
They said, "We'll open your ears.
We'll put a pillar where you stand.
You are the light of humanity."

Here is the ladder to reach You.
Here are the steps
Of that ladder to reach eternity.
Give the blessings of that destiny.
Entertain us at that stage.

Real life is your life.
Real death is yours.
This world is yours.
The next world is yours.
This is the reward given to the one
Who gives thanks to God.

Be silent my brother. Don't say too much,
Unless you have nothing else to do.
There is no place to hide
Where the wind of Love blows.

60.

Accept only the Lover,
The One who makes man fall in Love,
The drunk and intelligent Lover,
Into the assembly.
That drunk is such that
He cannot differentiate his belt from his hat.

Talk brings fights and war all the time.
Because of talk, men like Râfizî[124]
Argue with Ömer,[125]
And Ömer argues with Alî.[126]

Be silent! Cut talks short.
Watch the One whose face
Is more beautiful than the moon.
He is such a moon
That if He appears to the moon,
The moon will be split in two
Because of His light.

O moon-faced Master, cover Your face.
O Soul of Lover, exalt.
Give Your ecstasy to us
And watch us when we are out of ourselves.

148

61.

So, open the eye of the Soul
And look at the Lovers.
They're like the Heart.
It's an upside-down gathering,
An assembly that has no head, no feet.

They all keep working
Without earning, without profit.
They are all boiling like a kettle.
They are all without curtain and drapes.
Their Hearts are like a shield
In front of His commands.
Whatever comes, they accept.

Their Hearts are more cheerful
Than the garden and rose,
More free than the cypress.
They are above mind and thought,
Cleaner than the Fountain of Life.

They have passed
Through the waves of the blood's sea
Without getting smeared
With one drop of blood.
They are pure and clean.

They are in thorns, but like a rose.
They are in jail, but like wine.
They are in mud, but like Heart.
They are in night, but like dawn.

They are in air like particles.
The sun is like a robe of honor for them.
They step in mud,
But appear in the middle of the Heart.

You also become company, even for an instant,
To their Soul.
You drink their wine from their cup.
You become nice and drunk
And pass beyond good and bad
With their wine.

Enough now, son. Be silent.
Not every bird can swallow figs.
Parrots eat sugar.
For ravens, it's something else.

62.

Why did God bring us into this world?
To make an uproar.
His chain makes the crazy ones more insane.

How can we be saved from this Love?
Even the sky is on a big bow string.
It's stretched like Lovers, upside down.

It is amazingly beautiful, amazingly charming,
This Love which gives joy to our Soul.
Yes, every night, come in as a drunk
Without knowing yourself.
Come in through the door.

O Love, you took my patience, my decision.
You drank my blood.
Because of Your trials day and night,
I've been hidden like the dawn.
Neither my day nor night is apparent.

How can I hide from the Soul?
Even if I become very subtle and Soul-like,
He would see me in the land of Absence,
Even if I roll over in that land.

O One who becomes a treasure chest
In our absence!
O One who opens the door
To existence from Absence!
Aren't you the One who created us?
Aren't you the One
Who brought us from Absence?

Existence is good for You.
It's for Your drunk.
The ear of Absence is in Your hand.
Both are Your slaves, Your creatures.
Both accept Your command,
Put it at the top of their heads.

Demolish the house. Make the smart crazy.
Pour that wine into the glass, then offer it
So that both will be saved
From losses and dangers.

O agile, dependable Love,
A drunk is greeting You.
Accept his greeting.
Don't be stone-hearted.

Since You broke his hand,
Since You took his sleep,
Come and end his hangover.
Stop at the village of the drunks.

63.

The stars and that lovely sky
Both become drunk after seeing Your face,
Which is more beautiful than the moon.
O sweet Charmer, Your face is beautiful.
Your eyes, your brows are beautiful.
That different charm of Yours
Is beyond beauty.

The sky doesn't have a Soul of Leylâ[127] like You,
Nor a beautiful Mecnun like me.
In fact, the world has never seen
This kind of Leylâ and Mecnun.

The smart person will know
And will be a charmer
Who has Moses' Heart like You
And a beautiful Hârûn[128] like me.
But there won't be any resemblance to them
In this dark, muddy land.

O the pivot of seven mills,
You are a gold mine,
At the same time, a rare and precious thing.
O Jesus of the present time,
Come and cast Your spell on us
So we can come to life.

Since I am a whole, unpierced pearl,
Never mind raw, never mind mature.
I am asleep in Your shadow,
Under the spell of Your opium.

Is it no wonder that particles
Dance to Your melodies?
Right here, the Mount Sinai of Moses
Has also passed out of itself.
So has that beautiful writing.
Keep playing.

O Heart, in order to please Your Heart,
You gather gold, show Your talent.
But have You seen any Harun
After he gathered the gold
Who hasn't gone to the ground?

That money, that wealth
Looks beautiful at first,
But has no way to real beauty.
It looks like poison inside of the antidote,
Like the poison of a mountain snake.

It looks like a grave of infidels
Who are full of troubles
And covered with wounds inside,
Yet all dressed up on the outside
In black satin garments.

Your ears and looks are
Like *cim*,[129] your eyes like *sad*,
Your statute life *elif*
And Your eyebrows like *nun*.

Yes, because of all these letters of the alphabet,
I have become a student of reading and writing
On board Soul.
In that beautiful sea, I've become a boat
And turned into a sailor.

The arch of the sky's roof,
Which has the catapult of greatness,
Doesn't resemble me.
O Beauty who is balanced in every way,
Since I've fallen in Your love,
How can I be balanced?

O One who is the foundation
Of hundreds of states of drunkenness,
Yesterday You took the lead.
You asked me, "My indescribable beauty,
Are you happy in this world of wonder?"

The justice of Your face
Has cut the neck of every injustice.
The bad thing is
That he became drunk on his own blood
While you were gone
And found what he deserved.

O Shems of Tebriz,
You are such a great man
That there is no limit to Your greatness.
You are great
On hundreds of levels above greatness.
My Soul is such a fish
That there is a Jonah like You
Inside his belly.

64.

If you are in a deep, Heart-felt Love,
Suffer through the Beloved's grief and torture.
If you are not, go and pull thorns for nothing.

A Soul which looks like pure, clear pearl
Is necessary in order to find the way
To the Beloved.
Get that Soul out of Your body.
Put it on the gallows.

Sometimes he plunges in darkness.
Sometimes he wanders,
Becomes sick of that Soul
And covers him with words of disgust.

Don't look at yourself. Look at me.
Look and see: No trace of Soul is left on me.
Be as drunk as the nightingale.
Put all your belongings in the rose garden.

This violent, unruly horse of luck
Is not submissive to your Soul.
You are the fast cavalry of this temple.
Tame this horse. Control him.

You are a peerless horseman.
How long will you be a slave to the donkey?
The donkey tells you to carry a donkey's load.
Doesn't that shame you?

You are living under guilt like an Israelite.
You might as well put a sober, yellow fur
On your turban.

Or, in order to open your eyes,
Take some earth from the steps
On which Muhammad stood.
Put that on your eyes like salve.

65.

𝒥sn't it a strange thing?
We're in autumn,
But the sun has entered the sign of Aries.
My blood started to boil
In the river of body,
Danced like a camel
And made the body dance.

Watch the dances of the blood's waves.
See the valley full of Mecnun.[130]
Watch this unseen drinking,
Totally saved from the sword of death.

Even carcasses come to life.
The old get younger.
Even copper changes into pure smelted gold.
Better and more beautiful is coming,
Instead of the one who left our town.

This is a city full of abundance and drinks.
Every drunk has a glass in his hand.
Some offer more drink;
Others offer health, happiness.
This is a river of milk;
The other is honey.

There is only one Sultan in every town;
This one is full of Sultans.
There is only one moon in the sky;
This sky is full of Moons and Saturns.

Go. Go tell the doctors,
"You don't have any business there,
Because nobody gets ill there.
There is no sickness there."

This town has no judge,
No deputies, no rulers, no accounting.
Conflicts, animosities and fights
Can't walk on top of the sea.

66.

O Heart, You are such a kind, gracious Heart
That my beautiful One
Will find peace in the beauty of Your face.
O the One who is nice enough
To ask how my Heart is!
That kindness towards my Beautiful
Gives peace to my Heart.

We are alive because of Your kindness.
O Charmer to whom both worlds are submitted!
O the One who becomes Soul
To the name of Heart
With the life His name gives,
Make him alive!

The Heart becomes a circle around the body.
It embraces my body,
Wears the same mantle as my Soul.
In the end, both have been submerged in You,
O Beautiful, who does favors for the Heart.

O body of the One holding Heart's feet,
Here there is no mention of Heart's name,
No place for Soul.
On days after the Heart is brighter with You,
Nights are happier.

O the One who Loves me,
The One whom I Love!
Throw everything in the fire but Love.
You are like a dot in the body's *cim*[131]
And resemble the clearness in the glass of Heart.

The sound of drums keeps coming
From the temple of universal intelligence.
The sky's army is coming.
At this moment, it is announced that
"The Order of Heart is arriving."

The roads and plains are full of blood
From the swords of this army.
Having killed the enemy of that Sultan,
The road is drinking the blood of the Heart.

The head of the body's devil is crushed
By the attacks to the enemy line.
Sermons are delivered in the name of the Sultan.
The Council of State is filled
With the Order of the Heart.

O beautiful One,
Your words are as sweet as sugar.
Even Your ear-pulling is beautiful.
It's an award to hear from You,
Even if You look down on me.

If I didn't hide Your secrets,
I could tell so many things.
Then all people, top and bottom,
Would know the state of my Heart.

67.

Friends, spring has come.
We should go to the cypresses.
There we will wake up the fortune
Who keeps sleeping face down,
Like the fortune of the cypress.

We'll go to that strange land
By walking while our feet are tied,
Like the bride of grasses
Who runs without feet.
What a trick!

The name of the Soul
Who is freed from the land
Is going, flowing.
We'll pick up the Soul whose knees are tied
And take Him there.

O leaf, certainly you found the power
To split a branch and get out of the dungeon.
Tell us, tell us,
So we can do the same
And be freed from this jail.

O cypress, you came from the ground
And reached such a height.
What a spectacle the great One has shown you.
We want to know and see the same.

O bud, you came with the color
Of the rose beyond yourself.
How did you do that?
Tell us, so we can do the same.

Where is this white color?
From which direction
Is that smell of ambergris coming?
Where is the door to that house?
We will become the slave of the doorkeeper.

O nightingale, they come for your help.
I'll give everything for your song.
You are cheerful because of the rose.
I am cheerful because of you.
How can I thank you for that favor?

O cypress of the garden,
Turn into Hizir[132] who tells hidden secrets.
Tell them so I can put them up to my ears
Like earrings made of pearl and coral.

O nightingale, listen to the secret
From the rose garden.
Hear the truth without sound or alphabet.
If you understand this story,
You tune your voice and sing along.

The cooing of the dove has reached the Moon.
Parrots have gotten the sugar.
The Beauty is singing new songs;
We will make our Soul drunk with the melodies.

68.

Ⓞ Cupbearer of the One
Whose Heart is so bright,
Offer the glass of Your kindness,
Because that's why You brought us
From the valley of Absence.

Give the glass to the Soul,
That he would give up thoughts
And tear that curtain,
Because thoughts are harmful to the Soul.
Thoughts shorten life every moment.

O Heart, don't talk about Him.
Be silent. You wouldn't know His manners.
You look like a Moon,
But you don't have His mole on your cheek.[133]

That mole is the beauty
Of the man of knowledge and the wise.
But where are the eyes to see that
And the knowledge to understand?
Where is the rose garden that perfumes
And the nose to smell it?

The wine which in the end becomes a vineyard
Won't relieve the bitterness of the face.
Don't look for this wine.
Look for the other.
Where is the glass of grief?
Where is the glass of Cem?[134]

O Cupbearer whose face is so beautiful,
Offer us a wine that grows the flower of wisdom,
Nourished by the sea of Soul,
That comes and turns the inside of man
Into a bowl of pearls.

Pour on the head of the disbelievers
That big cup of wine.
Put that coldness in the fire.
Their no will turn into yes.

If there is no one in the assembly,
My words become greater.
Either turn into glory
Or stay away from us.
Don't reproach us.

You stick to the eyes like sores.
Turn the page, hodja.
Otherwise, I will break the pen.

The One who says, "Hey, hey,"
His Hey,hey comes from somewhere.
There must be some reason.
They don't raise the flag for nothing.
There must be either a king or an army there.

The Yurt[135] refuses to be empty.
Shake this body out of myself.
Free myself from this body.
The Soul that got stuck in the mud was drunk.
My feet are slipping.
I am afraid.

O Shems of Tebriz, O beautiful Helper,
Take care of us.
O the One who is the power of our feet
When we are walking
Is also health to our Soul
When we are sick.

69.

O Lovers, O Lovers,
I'll turn dirt into jewels.
O players, O players,
I'll fill your tambourines with gold.[136]

O, thirsty ones, O thirsty ones,
I will become the Cupbearer today,
Turn this barren land to Heaven,
Make it flow with the River of Kevser.[137]

O lonely ones, O lonely ones,
The time for salvation has come,
The time for salvation has come.
I will make every sufferer a Sultan, a Sencer.[138]

O unbelievers, O unbelievers,
I will open your locks,
Because I am absolute ruler.
I will make believers
Of whomever I please
And disbelievers of whomever I please.

O great man, O great man,
You are like a candle in Our hands.
If you are a dagger, I'll make you a glass.
If you are a glass, I'll turn you into a dagger.

You were a drop of sperm,
You became blood, then turned into a Beauty.
O human, come close to Me,
So I can make you more beautiful.

I'll turn sorrow into joy,
Make leaders out of the crazy ones.
I'll change the wolf to Joseph, poison to sugar.

O glasses, O glasses,
I opened My mouth,
Told My secret to make every thirsty mouth
Resemble the lip of the wine cup.

O rose garden, O rose garden,
When you make sweet basil
Equal to lilies,
Come to My rose garden, pick roses.

O sky, O sky,
When I make ambergris out of earth
And change thorns to flowers
Which smell like musk,
You'll be more astonished than the narcissus.

O Universal Intellect, O Universal Intellect,
Whatever You say, You are right.
You are the judge, You are the ruler.
I'll do better making less gossip.

70.

O Lovers, O Lovers,
I have lost the glass.
I have drunk the wine
Which cannot be contained by glasses.

I am drunk with the wine of Min Ledün.[139]
Go, complain to the judge about me.
I brought a taste of this wine
For you and the judge.

O Sultan of Truth,
Have You seen any double-faced ones like me?
I am alive with the live ones,
Dead with the dead ones.

With charmers, I will open up
Like a rose garden and smile.
With winter-like, cold disbelievers,
I become winter and turn to frozen ice.

O the one who wants bread, look at me.
God is my witness. I am drunk.
I don't know anything,
But neither have I turned around the jar,
Nor squeezed the residue of the grape.

I am drunk. Because of Him I sink,
But I sink in His river.
I have become rose marmalade
Because of His rose, because of His sugar.

Some day, Your face will be reflected
On my pale face.
I will shine like the Beauty of the land of Rum
And turn into a moon.
I won't be dark anymore.

I grabbed the cup of wine.
I shed the blood of thoughts.
I became one with the Beloved,
But you don't see me. I am behind the curtain.

I've hung thoughts,
Because thoughts keep man awake.
I'm tired of them. I'm confused because of them.

Time is my time.
The universe admires me.
My excursion into the land of Absence
Brought orders from the Khan of Truth.

There is another Soul in my body,
Another mind in my Soul,
A different touch in my Beauty.
I followed His trace. I reached Him.

If you tell me, "There is not much time left,
You have to go," I'll tell you,
"Tell this to the one who is alive:
I have given my life to my God.
I have been dead, long gone."

Be silent! The nightingale asked the falcon,
"Why do you keep silent? Why don't you sing?"
The falcon answered,
"You'll see me when the Sultan is hunting.
I'm better than a hundred soldiers."

71.

O the One who is with me like my Heart,
But is hidden at the same time,
Greetings to You.
You are the Kaaba[140] of my prayers.
Wherever I go, I turn toward You.
I want to reach You.

Wherever You are, You exist everywhere.
You look at us from a distance.
If I mention Your name,
The house is illuminated, even at night.

Sometimes like a tamed falcon,
I flutter my wings over Your hand.
Sometimes I come to a landing on Your roof
Like a pigeon.

If You are absent,
Why do You keep hurting my Heart?
If You are present,
Why do I set a trap in my Heart for You?

Your body is away from me,
But there is a window open
From my Heart to Yours.
From this window, like the moon,
I keep sending news secretly to You.

The sun, who is far away from us,
Is still sending its light.
O the Soul of everyone away from You,
I make my Soul a slave and servant to You.

I've been shining
The mirror of my Heart with You,
Making my ears like a book
To contain all the wonderful words
You've kindly said to me.

You're the one in the ears, mind and Heart.
What are all these things?
You are me. That's the way I praise You,
Explain You totally as a whole.

O Heart, in this adventure,
Didn't that Charmer say,
"If you are missing something,
I will complete it?"

O One who is the remedy for all trouble,
Look at, admire and see what kind of form
I'll put you in at this moment.

At times, I'll make you straight like *elif*.[141]
Other times, I'll bend and twist you
Like other letters of the alphabet.
One moment you become ripe, mature;
Another, I make you raw.

If you go for hundreds of years,
You are still in my hand, like a burnisher.
I'm the one who gives you joy
And the pleasure of things
Which are submitted by you.

O Sultan Husâmeddin Hasan,[142]
Tell the Beloved,
"I am turning the Soul
Into a sheath of knowledge for Your sword."[143]

72.

Verse 899

This time I really got involved with Love
And separated completely from devoutness.

I tore down my Heart.
I'm alive with something else.
I burned the mind from the bottom up,
Did the same with the Heart and thoughts.

O people, O people,
Don't expect me to act
Like an ordinary human anymore.
I fell in such reflection
That not even the insane
Could think my thoughts.

The insane have seen my craziness
And run away from me with foaming mouths.
I joined with death
And flew to the land of Nothingness.

My mind is totally annoyed with me today.
He tried to scare me,
As though I'd never seen him before.

Why should I be afraid of him?
I've dressed a different form for him.
How can I be a treasure?
I've been hidden in the corner.

I care neither for the bowl of stars
Nor the table of fortune.
For the poor, I lick so many plates
And fall in so much disgrace.

Because of the donkey's jealousy and evil eye,
I've been engulfed by blood
In the dungeon of flesh,
Dragging my bloody shirt on the ground.

I entered this world's jail for only one affair.
Otherwise, where am I?
Where is the jail?
Whose goods did I steal?

I am nourished by blood
Like an embryo inside the mother's womb.
Man is born once.
How many times have I been born?

Look at me carefully as long as you want.
Still you won't recognize me,
Because you haven't seen enough of me.
I have hundreds of attributes.

Get in my eyes.
Look at me through my eyes.
I have chosen a different mansion
Beyond the eyes.

You're drunk with wine.
I'm drunk without it.
You're a Lover with a smile.
But I keep smiling without mouth or lips.

I am such a funny bird
That when I was hungry,
I flew from the meadow into a cage.
There was no hunter, no trap.

With friends, a cage is better
Than the garden and meadow.
For the honor of Joseph,
I stayed at the bottom of the well.
I made my home there.

Don't cry because of the suffering He gives.
Don't complain because you're sick.
I've bought these troubles
By giving hundreds of sweet lives.

The silkworm keeps busy knitting silk.
Listen to me. I'm also a silkworm.
I keep knitting trouble,
Winding the silk of trouble.

I've been decaying in the grave of flesh.
Go to my Archangel,
Who will blow the last trumpet for me.
I will be resurrected.
I've gone to pieces
By sleeping in this grave of flesh.

No, you should close your eyes by yourself
Like an experienced falcon.
Don't say you dress in heavy garments
Like a peacock.

Kneel down in front of the doctor
And ask for an antidote,
Because in this mighty trap,
I've drunk so much poison, so much poison.

You'll be sweetened in front of the person
Who sells sweetmeats.
Your Soul will be light and sweet.
I haven't heard anything but, "Come on,"
From the Soul's sweetmeat.[144]

He makes you sweetmeat itself,
Which is better than giving it to you.
I haven't found any place
To get the taste or to hear of the sweetmeats
Except from His lips.

Be silent. While talking,
You may drop the sweetmeat from your mouth.
Like me, everyone else
Can get the smell without words.

Every unripened grape is yelling,
"O Shems of Tebriz, come help me.
I'm crying from tastelessness and immaturity."

73.

An image came to my eyes, saying,
"I've come from the rose garden of my Beloved
And the quarters of the Tavernkeeper.
Look at my sleepy eyes.

"I am the essence of drunkenness
And the wish and desire of existence.
I am the top. I am the bottom.
I've come like a whirling sky.

"From the beginning of creation,
I came to merge and get along with the Soul.
I went back, returned again,
Like a compass making constant turns
Around one point."

I said to him,
"Welcome. I hope you've come to help me."
He answered,
"That's the reason I've come here."

"I am the Moon. You are my light," he said.
"You are the rose garden and water.
I've come from a long distance,
I've come without shoes and without a turban.

"Though you are still immature, son,
You have a good name.
Don't be sad.
I've brought lots of favors for you.

"Come in with a smile.
Change this suffering.
O most Beautiful suffering!
Be cheerful.
I've come like thorns,
But I will give you roses."

The rose said, "Patience is the key to suffering,"
And He appeared on the rosebud,
And every branch moved, saying,
"Because I endured,
Now I come as scattering pearls."

74.

O Universal intellect,
Don't keep creating figures.
O Universal Soul, break your pen.
O searching man, don't look for footprints
On the surface of water.

O pure-hearted Lover,
Walk like pure, clear running water,
Because this still, waveless water
Adds Soul to Souls every moment.

Don't blame the still water
For getting ripples because of the wind.
Don't blame the water in the creek.
It has no fear, no worry.

See the design in emptiness,
The shape in shapelessness.
There are hundreds of colors
And smells in every shape.
Look at the food in fasting.
There is a garden of Eden
In every tree branch.

That form which destroys all forms
Is the source of Soul and Heart.
The body is melting because of its shame.
The Soul has escaped to the harem.

Because of His wine and His wind,
Many of His free creatures
Hold their breath like a mine and keep silent,
Filling their bellies.

Are you talking
About either the sea or the pearls?
Or about "Better judgement and fate
Will always prevail?"
You cannot solve anything with words.
Go, ride your horse under the flag.

Be aware, this is a funny, bizarre back road.
On this road, position and fame
Are at the bottom of the well.
When you arrive on the rough sea of blood,
Look for the dining table of kindness
Inside of the blood.

There is water in the fire.
Fire is hidden in the water.
The Soul is full of joy inside of His fire.
Soul falls in sorrow when it plunges in His water.

O One who gives all the blessings,
Keep our feet on dissent.
All comforts are discomforts without You.
All healths are illness without You.

75.

O sky, I learned this whirling
From the One whose face is like the moon.
I am a particle to His sun.
I learned this trembling, this dancing from Him.

O Beloved whose veil is the moon,
The river of Soul flows in His canal.
I learned how to run face down from that river.

The rose garden kept asking me
How I stole this musk gazelle.
I am such a lion that I learned to steal musk
From His gazelle.

I learned to tightrope walk so beautifully
Like a pumpkin vine
From this garden, this dried, twisted date palm,
From the curly hair
That has fallen on His forehead.

I closed my eyes and my mouth
To the world's pictures and designs.
I learned how to paint without smell or color.

His kindness, generosity and creativity
Opened my eyes.
I learned dying instant by instant
From the One who gives favor and compassion.

In sleep, you walk without direction.
Don't go six directions when you're awake.
Don't talk about direction.
I've found a side beyond directions.

76.

Really, we opened your door.
Don't separate your friends from yourself.
Don't send them away.
Don't worry about the one
Who separates Him from you.
Don't dirty your clothes. Stay clean.

Thanks to God, with the strength
Of the religion in which I believe
He did us a favor
And gave us the power to praise Him.
Don't close your door, then.

O friends, don't be sad.
I gave you wealth. I made you rich.
Don't deceive, don't cheat anyone.
I gave you strength and power,
Made your Heart brave.
Don't be afraid.
Don't love your name, your fame.

My God, open our Hearts.
Increase our dignity.
Show us our full Moon.
Don't worship self-made gods.

I don't have any God but Him.
Every creature has received His help,
His goodness.
His kindness kept His promise.
You don't deprive
The one who comes after you, either.

The words smell Heart,
And Heart appears from the words.
Say something which will be worth accepting.
Don't let the people around you down.

77.

O one who walked and has gone
As clean as the glass of Cem![145]
O one who is accused
Of the Love of the Moon-faced One!
This death will bring up your purity.
Don't worry that much.

O my dear, my Soul and your Soul
Are in the sea of blood.
Keep searching.
Let's see who's going to find the pearl.
Whoever finds it will come forward.

How could I possibly close my eyes
And lose hope, in the sea of pearl,
That every moment good news is coming
From the coast of the sea of Soul?

I became lazy after I fell in Love.
I gave up superiority,
Gave up being at the top of that leisure.
Because with the Love of the Sultan,
Top becomes bottom,
And bottom is considered top.

The sky of Heart has drunk wine from His table
And become pale.
When this Love saw me,
He recognized me and said,
"This is one who is from Us, separated from Me."

Look at my face, which goes from color to color
With the Love of the Sultan
Who doesn't change color.
Sometimes it looks like saffron
Because of His grief,
Sometimes red because of shyness.

I have slipped out of existence.
I am totally annihilated.
I've become the interpreter of God,
While sober or drunk.
Nobody can hear anything anymore,
Nothing less than His words.

I went to the bazaar in Egypt.
I entered the presence of a great person there.
I saw someone whose face resembles Joseph.
Then, by mistake, I asked his price.

The saint of Egypt said to me,
"You are in Love. I will give Him to you."
This must be either
An extraordinary favor from Him
Or His generosity and kindness.

I didn't appreciate that then.
I thought it was just a caprice.
I am so sorry now for my heedlessness.
I miss Him so much.

O the Beloved with His mighty power
Makes the impossible possible in two worlds.
I swear to God, there is no one
Who could ever realize things as you do.

O Tebriz, you get this honor.
"Way back in the time of Elest,"[146]
Before my praise to Shems,
The pen wrote this, and the inks have dried.

78.

Spring is here, friends.
Let's stay in the garden
And be guests to the strangers of the green.

We'll fly from one flower to the other,
Like bees making the six corners
Of this earth's hives prosperous.

An envoy came from this fortress
And said, "Don't beat the drum secretly.
With our yells, we would tear down the place
Where that Love's drum is beating."

Hear that voice which comes from the sky,
"Rise, all insane ones.
I sacrifice my Soul to the insane.
Let's scatter our Soul today."

Let's break all the chains.
Every one of us is a blacksmith.
Let's go to the fireplace where the pincers are.

Let's fan the flame of the Heart's fire
Like the furnace of blacksmiths
So we can have iron Hearts
Under our control with this breath.

We'll put fire in this universe,
Incite riots in the sky,
Make his sober, resisting mind
Turn around, become dizzy like ours.

We are like a ball, without hands and feet,
Sometimes at the end
And sometimes at the beginning of the square.
Who told you we could do what we want?
Who told you we are independent?

No, no. We are like a club
In the hand of the Sultan.
We send hundreds of thousands of balls
To His feet.

Let's be silent. Silence is made
With some material like craziness.
His mind is such a fire
That we hide this fire by wrapping it in cotton.

79.

𝔍 came again like a new Bairam.[147]
I came to break the door of the dungeon
And the teeth of fate,
Which are abusing and exploiting humans.

I came to put fire on the waters
Of the seven dry stars,
Which suck the blood of the people on earth.
I came to calm and extinguish their wind.

I flew like a falcon from the palace of the Sultan
Who has no beginning of the beginning.
I came to tear to pieces
The great eagle owl
Who eats the parrot in its ruined place.

I promised to give my Soul to the Sultan
Right at the beginning.
If I change my promise,
The back of Soul will be broken.

Today I am like Âsaf.[148]
The sword of order is in my hand.
I will cut the head of the rebels
In front of the Sultan.

If you see green for a few days
At the garden and field of those rebels,
Don't worry.
I will pull those plants up from their roots.

I won't harm anyone
Except the unjust, cruel tyrant.
I would be an unbeliever
If I touched the good Ones.

Wherever there is a ball,
The club of union rolls it.
With that club, I will break the ball
Which doesn't come to the field by the club.

I sat at His assembly.
I saw His favor, how He grabs His work.
I became His paid servant
In order to break the legs of the devil.

I was a small particle and became a mine
In the hand of the Sultan.
Make this very clear:
I got so heavy
That if you had put me on a scale,
The scale would have been broken.

How can you take home
Someone who is so drunk
That he falls on the ground as I do?
Don't you know
That I will break this, tear that?

If the watchman asks what I'm doing,
I pour the wine glass over his head.
If the doorkeeper tries to pull my hand,
I break his.

I will stop and pull the sky out by the roots
If it doesn't turn around Heart.
I'll break the neck of fate
If it becomes despicable.

You set the table of kindness
And invite me as Your guest;
So when I break a piece of bread,
Why do You pull my ear?

No, no, I am at Your table.
I am Your honored guest.
I will serve a glass or two of wine
To the guest so that he will overcome his shyness.

O the One who makes me say poems,
I'm afraid I will be rebelling against Your orders
If I close my mouth and keep silent.

I will walk without fear
And break the pole of Saturn
If I receive wine from Shems of Tebriz
And become drunk.

80.

O the One who becomes
The Moon and bright light to me,
Since I've seen Your face,
I'm full of joy wherever I stay.
It's a rose garden wherever I go.

Everywhere is a garden
If the reflection of the Sultan is there.
I set a table to drink
Wherever I arrive.

That Charmer whose face
Is more beautiful than the moon,
Rise from the land of Absence.
Put Your head through my window.
Come inside even if all the doors
In this six-door convent are locked.

He comes and says, "Hey, greetings.
I brought you hundreds
Of different kinds of appetizers.
I brought you hundreds of different kinds of wine.
I am the Sultan of Sultans.
I play melodies from Isfahan.[149]

"I am a bright sun.
I tear the curtains in such a nice way.
I am spring. I've come to remove the thorns.

"The One who wants the pleasure
Of drinking, joy and music day and night
Should know
That I am the taste of sugar, the oil of almonds."

"Please repeat that," I respond.
"Start giving favors and kindness again.
Tell me again why You're not sad.
I'm a little slow to understand.
I'm a little hard-of-hearing."

"That hard-of-hearing ear," He says,
"Is better than the others.
Your ears are one hundred times
Better than others,
Because there's air in others.
I am in your ear."

Go, go. You are stately, the Soul of life,
Pleasure and drink,
The angel at the gate of heaven.
You are heaven because You hold onto my shirt.

You are the mountain.
You are the phoenix, the strong rope.
You are the water and the giver of water.
You are my garden, my cypress, my jasmine.

Skies put their heads down in front of You.
Angels scatter their wings.
Heart tells You,
"I am wax for You; for others, iron."

81.

Yesterday, that Beloved
Put a golden crown on my head.
It doesn't matter how much You hit me.
The drunkenness of that wine
Doesn't leave my head.

The Sultan who sews the hat of eternity
Wears it at night.
He took it off His head
And put it on mine.
How can I say it will be eternal?

If I don't have a hat or a head,
The moon will turn out to be my head.
The pearl shines better
If it doesn't have a shell for a cover.

Here's my head. Here's a big hammer.
If you want to try, hit it.
If that head could be broken, rest assured
That I would be sweeter than the mind and Soul.

The walnut which chooses its shell
Usually stays empty.
How could it taste my Prophet's marzipan?

His marzipan is made
With walnuts, almonds and sugar.
It makes my mouth sweet
And, at the same time,
Gives light to my eyes.

Son, if you find what's inside,
You won't even look at the shell.
Wherever Jesus stands,
You don't look for the donkey.

How long will you talk about the Kullah?[150]
It's not a big deal
If one donkey is missing
Out of a bunch of donkeys.
Watch my big horseman;
Never mind the lean horse.

Power, strength and health come to the Lover
From the Beloved's strength,
Because the greatness of the Lover
Is from the greatness of my greater God.

O One who has fallen
Into all kinds of grief,
Don't say, "Ah, ah."
Say, "Allah."
O Joseph who is from the Soul,
Don't talk about the well.
Talk about glory and presence.

82.

O Love, you crack me into pieces like an idol.
I'll take you to the judge.
Nobody asked me to be a witness.
I am a witness, completely unindebted.

You are the One who is judged.
You are the judge.
You are the past.
You are the future.
You are the One who gets into a rage.
You are the One who is contented.
You appear different with every moment.

O my beautiful great Love,
You are me. I am You.
You are the torrent.
You are the heap of grain for threshing.
You are joy, suffering and grief,
All at the same time.

These are from You. Those are from You.
You are pure from this and from that.
You are these plains. That mountain is You.
You are the valley of kindness.

You are the sweetness and drunkenness
Of close ones.
You are the sea full of pearls
And the mine full of gold and money.

You are the love of talking
And the passion of silence.
Comprehension is You. You are also ecstasy.
The right way, justice and reproach are all You.

O the One who became Sultan
To the Sultan of Sultans!
O mind, O the One
Who put His throne at the land of Soul!
O the One who offers hundreds of signs,
Still His face, His trace are unseen!
O the sea, the store of Absence!

For You, all the beauties and ugly ones
Are like a picture in front of Your brush.
If You desire it, You draw a beautiful picture.
If You want to draw ugliness,
Then You tear and throw them
To sickness and death.

If the pictures knew
They all came from the same pen,
They would get along fine with each other.

Your zeal says, "Go away,"
To the ones coming toward you
To give their Soul.
Your kindness invites them by saying,
"Yes, come here."

But Your kindness exceeds
And attracts the Lover more and more.
Like light is superior to darkness,
Your favor is much greater than Your grief.

He hooked everyone with one desire, one fancy
And kept pulling them behind Him
From place to place.
You are the One.
The flag in Your hand pulls the army of all fancies.

At first, you give desire for ownership, for power.
Then you give another fancy
And grab greatness from the one
To whom You have given it
And make him a slave to the other.

Every moment, a desire
Comes from the land of Soul to the body
Without the knowledge of the One
Who divides destiny and says, like a child,
"This is mine. This castle is mine."

I'll be silent. I'll close my mouth
So that this world won't become
Mixed up and confused.
You cannot be explained with words.
What can I say, more or less?

84. 151

Verse 1029

*T*his world has no patience, no consistency.
How long should I decide to stay in this mud?
My Beloved doesn't even need my Love.

I am not the black topsoil
Just so the wind can blow me to dust.
I am not the roof of the sky
Just so I can wear a gray mantle.

Since He is my store, my bazaar,
Why should I rent a store?
I am the Sultan of Soul.
Why should I watch and serve like a servant?

I will tear the store down.
My store is His Love.
I have found the mine of ruby.
How can I be a shopkeeper?

I don't have a cut on my head.
Why should I wear a bandage?
I am the doctor of the world.
Tell me, why should I look sick?

I am the nightingale of the garden of Heart.
It would be a shame to become an owl.
I am a rose sapling in His rose garden.
It would be bad for me to be a thorn.

I should stay away from troubled ones,
Since I am close to the Sultan.
I should be disgusted with my self,
Because I have reached His Love.

If I look for a job to do,
He ties my hands with chains.
If I intend to stay sober,
He drowns me in a jar of wine.

O hodja, I am a glass of wine.
How could I bring sorrow to the Heart?
I am the candle light.
How could I darken the house?

Come one night. Be my guest.
I'll put the full moon in front of you.
Give your Heart to me.
I'll do all the favors and take your Heart.

If you lose your life in Love,
I'll become your life, your Love.
This will be enough for you.
If the thief steals your turban,
I'll become a turban for you.

Don't give your Heart to others.
You can't find a pearl like me.
Come in slowly. Don't worry.
I'll worry for you.
I'll be responsible for you.

I've overcome laziness and boredom.
I've cleared my Soul of fear.
Death won't come unless it's at the given time,
Yet I command death. He listens to my orders.

My thanks to His pleasures.
My patience to His disasters.
O Cupbearer, get up.
Give me wine so that I will be drunk.

The wine is the wine I boiled. I made it.
Joy and pleasure are the ones
I have brought as good news.
My grape is ripe.
Why should I crush unripe grapes?

O the experienced player
Plays his tune until dawn.
As long as my head is like that, healthy,
Why should I be turned into a carcass?

You are a night bird tonight
Or in the arms of a beauty.
Stay awake like a fairy.
Stay awake and watch me dance.
I'll tell you all about everything.

I swear to God, our foundation is enforced.
Our evidence becomes obvious.
Thanks to God, I am a lion, not a hyena.

Joy and pleasures have come.
Sorrows are all gone.
Thanks to God, Who gives favors and kindness,
O customer, kneel down so I can buy you.

I've been playing the tambourine since dawn.
I have had a wedding.
I will throw the veil in the fire.
How long should I stay covered?

I've withdrawn myself
Like dawn from the sky,
Which is covered by a veil.
I will be the omnipotent of the universe.
I will repair all broken Hearts.

The homeless have the house.
The poor have the wealth.
Be silent! If you are silent,
I will talk for you.

If I have the same disposition
As Shems of Tebriz,
If we have the same star,
I will shine in six dimensions.
I will be enlightened in six dimensions.

85.

𝔍 tried very hard to become
The mirror of virtue and goodness,
But as much as I tried,
You made me a tavern, a town of wine.

I became a private tavern for special ones
In order to be a doctor and cure diseases
And mend all the broken bones.
I became a sea for divers.
I became a whole sun.

You made forms of angels in this world of mud
Just so they would be charmers.
You exalted them.
You threw me away
In order to make me the elixir of closeness.

You set a flame for the way of Hârût,[152]
Taught magic to lots of people.
As for me, You made me a candle
To enlighten the darkness.

The Turk always acts like a Turk,
The Tacik[153] like a Tacik.
I become a Turk one moment
And a Tacik another.

Sometimes I become the crown of the Sultan,
Sometimes the tricks of the devil.
One moment I become the smartest of minds,
Other times, a child
Who plays the game of tipcat.

In order to become the rose color of Your face,
The fineness of Your hair,
I shed the blood of duality,
Merge and unify with only Joseph.

86.

J will never kick out the drunk
Who has fallen down at my door.
If I have wine in my house,
I'll put it in front of him.
I'll sit and drink with him.

My drunk guest is my Soul, my crown, my Sultan.
I put him on top of my head.
He is that holy to me.

O my friend, my confidant, make me drunk.
I don't count the day that I am not quite drunk
As part of my life.

Since I sacrifice my life like gold
To the Cupbearer,
I don't look at anyone's face
But the Cupbearer's.
I don't listen to anyone but the Cupbearer.

How much more shall I try myself,
This smart, this wise Soul?
The day I am drunk,
I am like a ship sailing around.
The day I am sober, I stand still with an anchor.

Where is the wine for the body?
Where is the wine for the Soul?
Where is the sky? Where is the rope?[154]

There is a drunk who vomits.
There is a drunk who brings distance near,
Who passes over all the roads of earth.
One is despicable on earth;
The other, highly esteemed in Heaven.

O Caravan Master, if You are drunk,
If Your Heart is bright,
Don't sleep tonight.
Be silent. Be silent.
O One who is all kindness,
Drink from this wine.

87.

$\mathcal{P}$ull yourself together. Come to your senses.
Don't look so confused.
The One from Mecca knows I am from Batha.[155]

The color of my face is turning to saffron
Because of that Heart-catching,
Tulip-faced Beauty.
Every moment my business is growing
Because of that Beauty, adding joy to my joy.

My Heart resembles the snow,
Melting every moment,
Wanting to be there all the time,
Because I am from there.

People are happier
Where there is a more orderly life.
Come and look at me.
I've become crazy from the calls
Coming from Soul.

That snow says, "I am melting
Every moment to become a torrent,
A cascade running to the sea.
I am from the sea. I am the sea."

I stay alone, stand still,
Freeze and become lifeless.
I have been chewed
Between the teeth of trouble.

Untie your knots, like water,
So that you'll be saved
From the torture of those teeth.
I will be tightly knotted.
Naturally, I'll be chewed up, crushed, beaten.

Come to your senses.
Leave the snow's water alone.
Look at the real wines. They are boiling up:
"We are sharp and could cause lots of trouble."

I talk too much.
You know I know only that much.
I'm like a reed flute without a head or feet
In the hands of the flute player.

I become more exuberant every moment,
Foam and froth.
I am flying like a mind without wings,
Because I am from the heights.

If you are tired of me,
Look at the Sultan of time.
See Him so He can give you wisdom.
That Beauty of a halvamaker makes you sweet.

O Beauty, the One who is existence
To the ones who deny existence!
O the cure for the ill ones!
O the One who says, "I am from Kafdagi,[156]
I belong to the phoenix and make the Soul fly!"

Enough. I'll be silent, stop staying all this.
But He won't stop.
He keeps saying all these words.
In fact, I'm like a parrot.
His Love is sugar.
I start talking because of His sugar.

88.

O my Beloved, O my Beloved!
O the One who doesn't know mercy!
O my Charmer, the One who took my Heart!
O my confidant, the One who relieves my grief!

O the One who becomes a moon
For us on earth!
O the One who becomes dawn
In the middle of the night!
O the One who becomes a shield for us
In the moment of danger!
O my cloud which rains sugar for me!

How beautifully You flow in my Soul.
How beautifully You cure my illnesses.
O my religion, O my faith,
O my sea full of pearls!

O the torch for night passengers!
O the chain for crazy Lovers!
O the Kible[157] for everyone!
O my Caravan Master!

You are a brigand and, at the same time, a guide,
A Moon and, at the same time, Jupiter.
You are on this side
And, at the same time, on the other one,
The corner where I stand,
The place on which I rely.

You came like the prophet Joseph,
Looking for a customer.
You've come to burn my Egypt, my bazaar.

You are the Moses of my Mount Sinai,
The Jesus who cures all my illnesses.
You are the halo of my light.
You are my Ahmed-i Muhtar.[158]

You are company for me in the dungeon,
Sometimes my smiling prosperity.
I swear to God
That You are hundreds of times more than that.
O my Beloved, who deserves more praise
Than my many, many praises!

You tell me, "Jump over to this side."
"How can I come to Your temple?" I ask.
You answer, "O my deceitful one, O my creature,
Don't try to find excuses."

I say, "You are an unmeasurable treasure
Who deserves Sultans."
"Yes," He answers, "but it is not free.
I want Soul, special Soul."
I say, "I agree, take the weight from me."

If you want treasure, put up your head.
If you want Love, give your Soul.
Come in rank. Don't return,
O my Hayder-i Kerrar.[159]

89.

Ｏ gardener, autumn has come,
Autumn has come.
See the sign of sorrow of the Heart
On the leaves and branches.

O gardener, listen carefully.
Hear the cry of the trees.
There are hundreds of Souls
Wailing silently everywhere, hundreds of Souls.

Eyes won't tear without a cause.
Lips won't become dry without a reason.
Nobody's face becomes pale like saffron
Without suffering like saffron.

In short, the raven of grief
Has landed in the garden, asking,
"Where, where is the rose garden?"

Where is the iris? Where is the August rose?
Where is the tulip, the cypress?
Where is the jasmine?
Where are the beauties
Who dress the green of the grasses and meadows?

Where is the taste of the fruit?
Where is all the free honey and milk?
All the Hearts and lungs are dry,
Longing for milk.

Where are the nightingale's sweet melodies?
Where is the coo of the dove?
Where are the arrogantly beautiful peacocks?
Where are the parrots? Where?

After eating a grain, just like Adam,
It seems they've left the house of heaven.
Their crowns have been blown off their heads
With this test.
Their dresses have fallen
Because of it.

The rose garden has fallen into deprivation,
Just like Adam.
It cries and at the same time waits, saying,
"Don't abandon hope of the One
Who has all kindness and favors.
Don't give up."

All the trees draw a line.
They are all mourning, dressed in black.
They don't have even one leaf.
They have nothing left.
They are crying, yelling because of this test.

O stork, O head of the village,
Please answer my question.
Where did you go, underground
Or over the sky? Over the sky?

"O villainous raven," they say,
"That water will flow again to the rose garden.
The world will be filled
With color and smell again,
Just like heaven. Just like heaven."

O raven, who talks only nonsense,
Wait for only three months.
You'll see the festive days of earth.
Festive days will come again in spite of you.

With the sound of our Isrâfîl,[160]
Our oil lamp will shine,
We will come back to life from death.
We will find new life
From that merciful Soul
That resembles the sun.

How long will this denial, this doubt last?
You are a mine of beauty.
You have taste, charm.
Ascend to the sky like the pupil of the eye,
Without stairs.
Fly to the sky like sight, without stairs.

Monster autumn is dying.
You kick its grave.
Guard, guard right now.
A kingdom is borning.

O morning, light up the world.
Expel the Indians. Warm up time.
Cast spells. Cast spells.

O sun who does all good,
Come to the sign of Aries.
Don't leave any ice or mud.
Spread ambergris, ambergris.

Fill the rose garden with laughter.
Bring life to the dead.
Light up the day of judgement.
Do it now, clearly. Do it now.

Seeds are freed from their jail.
We're also freed from inside our houses.
The garden has brought hundreds of gifts
From the land of Absence, hundreds of them.

The rose garden is filled with hundreds of roses.
Gossip stops.
Time starts giving birth.
Time becomes the father and helps to give birth.

The stork lands
On that great big house like the sky,
Saying, "Leylek."[161]
O the One whose help is asked, is begged,
It's Your property, Your property.

The nightingale is playing its lute,
The dove is saying, "coo-coo,"
And the other birds come
As players of young destiny.

I am so loaded with this tumult
That I can hardly talk. I'll stop.
In fact, it's impossible to explain
All the thoughts in my Heart
With words.

Be silent. Listen.
New news is coming
From the garden, from the birds.
An arrow has come flying
From the land of Absence.

90.

O Lovers, O Lovers, it's time
To leave this world.
I hear the sounds of the exit drums
With the ear of my Soul.

Here, right now, the Caravan Master is up,
Sets the string of camels and asks his fee.
Why have you slept all this time,
O people of the caravan?

The sounds which come from the front and back
Are the sounds of departure,
Sounds of the bells
Hanging on the necks of camels.
Every moment, Soul and breath
Appear in the land of Absence.

A bunch of amazing people
Came from the light of upside-down oil lamps
And from behind the deep blue curtains
To reveal the secret things.

You fall in deep sleep
Watching the wheel of the sky.
Cry for this life which has passed so quickly.
Wake up from that deep sleep.

Everywhere there are torches and candles,
Lots of noise and lots of action,
Because tonight the world has become pregnant.
The eternal world will be born.

You were earth and became Heart.
You were ignorant, but you learned much.
The One who pulls you here
Now pulls and drags you over there.

Don't make a face at Him.
His fire is like water.
His pulling, His other unpleasant things
Are very good.

His job is to sit on Hearts.
His fun is to break the repentant.
Even the hearts of particles are trembling
From His innumerable deceits.

O this sarcastic smile
That jumps out of the slit of the mouth,
O the boasting that says,
"I am the head of the village,"
How long will you be jumping around?
Give up. Bend your neck, your head.
Otherwise, they will pull and bend you like a bow.

You kept sowing the seed of deceit,
Lamenting and denying God.
Now let's see you, O charlatan.

O donkey, better eat hay.
You deserve a black pot.
O the shame of your house, your family,
It would be better if you pass under ground.

I have another person in me.
These angers come from him.
If water burns, it's because
It's boiled from the fire.

There's no stone in my hand.
I don't fight or argue with anyone.
I'm as pleasant as the rose garden.

My anger is because of him, from that world.
The one who is angry isn't me.
He is the one who jumps
From one side to the other.
I sit at the threshold, moving nowhere.

The one who sits at the threshold
Is mute, but talks.
You give this hint. It's enough.
Be silent.   Don't say anything else.

91.

Who is He? Who is He?
He is the One who makes Lovers crazy, insane.
The earth becomes more beautiful than the sky,
With His light.

He is the One
Who guides the Soul away from himself,
The jewel of treasures,
The cypress of the garden,
The Archangel Gabriel himself.

He is the drunkenness
Of the Soul and universe,
The Beloved of the eyes and mouth.
He is the looter of profit and stores,
Abstinence from sins and religion.

The moon and sun are ashamed
After seeing Him.
He is a stone Heart who spreads pearls,
Such a tyrant, that even iron mountains
Are fragmented by fear of Him.

The sun has become richer because of Him.
Hundreds of moons are eating
Like the flying vulture star[162] at His harvest.

Come, O Soul of eternity,
Come, O beautiful face,
Come, O sun of dawn,
Come, O One who is understanding and light.

Come and shine on the faces.
Water the field of Hearts.
Take off your shoes and sit at the head of Souls.

O knowledge, go away.
O ear, hear the good news.
O mind, get drunk.
O eyes, watch the kingdom.

The eyes of Job are opened.
The son of Jacob has returned.
The sun has become a peer to the moon
And sits at the drinking table.

I used to make purses;
I was burning with greed for gold.
I shouldn't appear poor anymore;
I saw treasure at the ambush.

O the One who has the best writer
Of the order of "Reveal,"[163]
O the One in front of His mind,
The universal Soul has become
Like a child biting his nails.

The knowledgeable One who sees Him
Increases his knowledge a hundred fold.
He raises his hands above his head
And clapping, says,
"What a wonderful helper!"

Under the shade of His lotus tree
Man became the Archangel Gabriel.
It is not everyone
Who has a plump calf at his guest house.

He has found the way to God's table,
Has understood, become one
With the spiritually chosen Ones.
Black-eyed Houris[164] carry plates full of blessings.

How long will you be reading
The book of the Soul's secret with banal people?
This book is obviously reaching
The hands of the right people anyway.

92.

Who is He? Who is He?
He must be a second Joseph
Or maybe Elijah, Hizir[165] or the Fountain of Life.

This must be a divine garden,
The assembly of God,
The salve of Isfahan,[166]
Or the Glory of God,
Devoid of all deficiencies.

He is the One who adds Soul to Soul.
He is the Heaven of Me'vâ.[167]
He is our beautiful Cupbearer,
Our wine of Soul.

This resembles sugar cane.
The mouth of the Beloved
Looks like a head in Love.
This resembles that silver statue.
This is joy and pleasure,
Ease and happiness.

We are drunk today.
O my Father, we broke our repentance.
O my Father, we came out of famine.
This day gives the most abundance of the year.

O player who has the voice of David,
Throw all my belongings in the fire.
Hit the high and low notes;
It's time for singing and playing.

I am Your drunk, Your ruined one.
I depend on Your rule.
I am Your sacrifice, Your Isaac.
That is the fate of sacrifice.

We're free from fear, from hope.
Where is Love? Where is modesty and shyness?
It's hell for the one who's ashamed;
This is the time to leave all shame behind.

Look at the red and yellow roses.
See this instigation, this disorder.
Watch the dust under the sea.
All these are from Imran, son of Moses.

He changes every substance into Soul,
Makes the Soul know God,
And turns everyone into Solomons of justice.
This must be holy order, a rule of giants.

Love, where is all Your nonsense talk,
That joy, that drink, that beauty?
No one understands You, not even one man.
They think it's Syriac.[168]

The brilliant sun is coming,
Swaying like a drunk,
Like a Sultan coming with a ball and club.

Whenever there is a ball,
It always rolls with a club.
You also become handless and footless.
This is the time for union.

If you become a ball, without hands and feet,
His club will become a foot for you.
You will go to the temple of God,
Because this is a divine journey.

That water runs into the river.
Now throw your jar on the stone.
Prostrate yourself, don't say anything,
Because this is the assembly of the Sultan.

93.

Don't go there.
Come here, O my smiling sapling rose,
O one who is the mind of my mind,
The Soul of my Soul.

Look this way. Come to our side.
Exalt in the sugar cane,
O my Fountain of Life.

I want to come to you secretly
After the darkness of night has fallen.
Your face will lighten up the night
For night travelers.

In relation to your Love, who am I?
I'm the cupbearer for your bloody tears.
My eyes are a jar of wine.
My eyelashes are the filter for the wine.

I'm serving You wine from my tears,
My Heart is roasted.
These are the only things I have.

The sea of my eye won't be deprived of that pearl
For even one moment.
Your beautiful ruby will always
Stay in my mine.

Even with all this,
Where is your gratitude?
What happened to your oath?
Give up this oppression and cruelty,
O my Beautiful.

Look! My eyes are tearing.
My face is pale,
Trying to reach your agate-colored lips.

God wrote on your face,
"Renew your faith."
My faith has been increasing
Because of your beautiful face and this writing.

When You're angry,
Your eyes tell such words to my eyes;
They belong to my secret fire.

He says, "Don't be afraid of that Beauty's anger.
Don't give up out of coyness.
First, drink a cup of His wine with sediment
And watch the end of this affair.

"There is a thorn for every rose,
There is a snake at the top of the treasure.
My Soul will reward you
For your patience and suffering."

After I heard these words, I said,
"Since you want to torture me,
Your suffering is my treasure."
I am like Abû-Hurayra;[169]
Your grief, your troubles
Become my leather bag.

I pick up things from the bag,
Make the beggar a Sultan.
I give gold and silver to the people who ask,
Because the full moon became my guest.

I pull out from the bag
Whatever my Heart desires.
This way, color comes to my face,
And blessings come to my table.

He said, "You are right.
Put your mind in your head.
Don't lose the bag.
You've found a good key,
O my trustworthy doorkeeper."

Patience is the key to affliction and troubles.
Patience is the ladder of rank and ascension.
Patience is the antidote of depression,
O my Arabic-reading Turk!
O my Beauty who knows Arabic!

Quit saying Lâhavle.[170]
O son, it's enough,
Because the devil of wine
Has become furious.
I quit Lâhavle,
And my devil starts saying Lâhavle now.

94.

For some time I've been left on this journey
With the sound of 'start the journey.'
For some time I've heard the sound of go,
But I've lost the location of my tent.

When will you save me
From the voice that says things like,
"Go, get on the road,"
So that I can reach You, Your glory,
My Beauty whose face is like the moon,
The place of my harvest? 171

O my Beloved! The One
Who is the light of the sun!
I've been happy with Your Love
On the journey through mountain and valley,
Plain and river, day and night.

But how is my road to be opened?
Where is that face? Where is that Sultan?
Tell me about that.
Tell me, tell me that.
I've been burned
By my desire for that Sultan.

How long will I be asking for Your news
From the morning breeze?
How long will I be searching through the image
Of the fish in the well's water?

I've been burned hundreds of times,
Flowered with the kindness of spring.
In all cases, I have admired the art of God.

95.

Yesterday, my Beloved's image
Was turning around the Heart.
I said, "Come in, lighten up my insides
With the light of Your face."

O Sultan of Sultans,
O the One who threw
My sane Soul into the fire!

O the One whose spring made my life green!
My Soul and many others all have wondered
At the things I've done.

O the One who is the Soul
Of the angels in the sky,
O the one who is the rosary
Of the fish in the sea,
There is a taste and trace of You
On every Beauty and beautiful face.

You are the greatest of the great.
The proof of every prophet,
You reign and, at the same time,
Are the source of justice.
You are also the remedy
To my irremediable disease.

My earth turns into golden treasure
With the brightness of Your sun.
With Your light,
My wandering thoughts gained wings.

I am full of melodies
In the arms of Your favors, like a harp.
Strike gently, so my strings won't be broken.

When the kindness of Your spring
Reflected on the garden of Soul,
Either the thorns disappeared in the rose,
Or all my thorns became roses.

This blood-drinking Heart
Set hundreds of golden tables every night
Because of the grace of Your face.

The specter of my Beloved comes every night,
Puts out His hand and scratches my head.
In the end, that Beauty who patted my head
Took my turban away.

The One who brought me from Absence
Made me talk every moment.
In the end, the One who made me talk
Became all the words I have spoken.

96.

If the rose with its beauty,
The jasmine with its fine three petals
See Your face, reach You,
They all grow so big, so beautiful.

O my Beautiful, life is Your rose garden.
O my Beloved, the wound You open
Is luck and prosperity for me.
To be a slave to Your slave
Is higher than being a king or sultan.

"I offer you life," You said.
No, no. Say, "I kill you," so that I will be brighter
And more alive, like a candle with its wick cut.

What do the devout look for?
Your mercy.
What do Lovers search for?
Your wound, Your oppression, Your cruelty.
He is death, dressed;
Others are alive in their coffins.

One runs for his life;
The other One sacrifices himself to Love.
One keeps his head down to save his life;
The other becomes an enemy to himself.

O the One who shines in my Soul
Like a Sun entering the sign of Aries!
O the One who turns me into
Yemen's[172] ruby with the light of His face!

97.

I merged so completely with Love,
Was so fused, that I became Love
And Love became me.
That way, I was saved
From instigations, trials, tribulations.

Yes, with complete Union,
Man becomes strange to himself.
There wouldn't be any animosity
If people could solve this problem.

There is a sea that isn't far from us.
It's unseen, but not hidden.
It's forbidden to talk about,
Yet, at the same time,
A sin and sign of ungratefulness not to.

To talk about Him
Is like comparing Him to a human.
To keep silent denies His omnipotence.
This is a problem with no solution,
A disease which has no cure.
You save us, O One who has kindness and favors.

The shapes, colors, smells of this world
Ask for His help every moment,
Just like a baby who doesn't know Him,
Yet wants nourishment from Him.

The Heart is asleep.
At the same time, He is awake,
Boiling up constantly.
He is like a lidded saucepan
That sits on top of the fire.

O the One who offers that wine
Without saying words to us!
Every moment a legend comes with a shout
Out of that silence.

There are hundreds of pities in Your curse,
Hundreds of generosities in Your greed,
Hundreds of bits of knowledge in Your ignorance.
He talks silently, like one surmises.

The words You said when You were silent
Are heard by the Ones
Who fell in Love and lost their minds.
I am in silence, but I'm exuberant with You.
I look like the Sea of Aden.[173]

Your Grace is doing Godliness,
Grants all wishes.
My God, help the one who is separated from You
To pass through himself.

O the One who is our consent, our coyness,
Our origin and our beginning!
How can the father of Hasan[174]
Know this secret of ours?

O the One whose Love buys us,
Pulls us from others!
O the One who tears our clothes,
Put Your hand on our torn dresses!

231

O the One who sheds the blood of my mind
Smuggles the patience out of my Heart.
O the One who merges with my Soul
Breaks the Soul of every shape!

If a bird flies away from the place
Where the Lover was ruined
And finds that his prey is dead,
It will keep tearing its coffin.

98.

The fortune of my Beauty never sleeps.
Neither do my eyes see sleep.
O the One whose beauty
Is a candle to this world,
My eyes become the basin for that candle.

With the food of Your Love,
Eyes and Heart have ceased sleeping.
They're nourished with Your Love.
Both of them, like a cypress,
Suck the juice of Your kindness
Without the need of a mouth.

The occupation of the Soul
Is not a bunch of nonsense.
The sustenance of Soul is not dirty.
It doesn't lose the state of canonical purity.
There is new form and shape born
Without man or woman
Every moment in the town of the Soul.

Every form is more beautiful than the moon,
Sweeter than sugar or honey.
They dress differently,
With hundreds of thousands of clamors,
And serve my Beloved.

They all admire the sovereignty of dervishes.
The water of the sky flows in their rivers.
O Heart, You came to their quarter as a drunk.
Clap Your hands.

Because of that charming Beauty's face,
Whose forehead is as bright as the Moon,
Earth turned into sky.
Help us, O Moslems, save us
From these designs filled with instigations.

99.

Suddenly, I catch a smell.
Maybe it's coming from my Beloved.
Maybe my faithful, drunk Beauty
Is drinking wine and remembering me.

O the Charmer
Who stays in my Heart and Soul,
How can He not remember me?
How can I be out of His Heart?
He's making Macun[175] for my broken Heart.

Now, because of this exuberance,
God's compassion is flowing
Like a cascade in my sea of secrets,
Like the river of Ceyhun.[176]

My act, my talk
Are the curtains of my ecstasy.
My Heart, which resembles a rose garden,
Is shamed by my thoughts,
Which look like thorns.

Where is the shout and sound
Which deserves my Love?
Where are the moon and sun
That have brighter lights than I do?

Leave this alone.
Now a Kaiser comes to Ethiopia
From the land of Rum
To clean away my rust,
To instigate trouble among the blacks.

Climb His roof and watch.
His news is coming from the Heart's window,
Hitting my Soul,
Which is fed by fire.

How can I talk about meeting Him?
How can I describe His Beauty?
Those parrots don't even come close
To the trap of my words.

Don't look at my Beloved
With the worth of my words.
Watch the Mount Sinai of Moses
On the Heart of my ideas.

My awake Beloved will give a hint
With these words
To the ones who are awake.
Tonight He will give a sign.

I wonder why this elephant with insomnia
Sees India in its dream.
Leylâ[177] came by,
Searching for her beloved in my Heart,
Which became Mecnun.

Tonight, all the earth will be washed away
From the torrent of my Heart,
Because the Source of my rivers is flowing
Through my Heart's canals.

He screams in my ears in such a way
That every particle
Becomes drunk with the sound.
I hear the sound of my flying Cafer's wings.[178]
I understand that he keeps flying.

My God, give another language to my Soul
Besides this one
So that when talking about Union,
My shingles won't untie.

You took the patience and decisions
From my Heart.
You made me drunk and threw me to the ground.
Where is my knowledge?
Where is my mind
Which used to understand everything?

Son, cover this
So that beautiful silver statue won't hear.
Beside Him, everything, including Soul,
Is a stranger to me.

O my peerless Beauty! O the One
Who is impossible to describe with words!
O the One whose quality
Cannot be contained with words!
O the One who covers my sins,
Give some beauty to these words.
Adorn these words.

O parrot with whom we are fed
At the same table,
Don't chew any sugars
Except the unconditional, uncircumstantial ones.
Don't talk about existence,
Attributes, signs, forms.

My Heart and Soul stay away
From faith and blasphemy.
They go only one way.
It would be hell for me
If I had anything else to do but You.

How can I beat the drum of others
While my table is full of Your sugars?
O One who has hundreds of musks
In every curl of His hair,
Who gives perfume
To hundreds of perfume sellers!

Son, put me up as your guest.
This is my food and drink;
This is my garden and field;
This is my gold and silver.
Play that tune until early dawn.

My Heart which has been sleeping is awake.
The One who has been drunk all night long
Is sobered
By a lightning strike to my Heart
From my clouds full of rain.

O One who has become
An admonition to my eyes!
The eyes of all the ones
Who came before or after
Have never seen a Love like this.

Many times I've become stone,
Many times pearl.
I've became a believer, then a disbeliever.
In this appeal, in this transformation,
Sometimes I was the head, sometimes the feet.

I'll go out of myself for one single day,
Give up good and bad
And start naming the attributes of God,
The One whom everyone needs,
The One who doesn't need anyone.

O the Owner of this watering sky,[179]
My Soul hasn't gotten any joy from it,
O my rose-faced One, O my rose garden,
My heaven and my flowers.

What is the night?
Hundreds of years have passed.
This fire hasn't been extinguished.
This hell hasn't cooled down.
I've turned into water with my shame,
But this fire keeps burning.

Every moment I become younger,
Keep hiding from myself.
This sound, straight kingdom
Makes me more beautiful, more attractive.

Since I'm part of the Soul,
I'll be the whole Soul.
Since I'm the thorn of the rose.
I'll be the rose.
I've become "we have heard."[180]
At the time my Beauty
Transforms me from one stage to another,
I'll become the words 'to tell.'

O the one who claps his hands for me,
Don't be confused.
O the one who plays for me,
Don't be tired.
There will be a day when
My Sultan will ask for your excuses.

There will be a day when you'll be His drunk.
There will be a day when you'll kiss His hand,
A day when you'll be scattered like my turban.

O Beautiful for whom my Soul became Ferhad,[181]
My Soul remembered Him tonight.
The strings of the harp are broken.
Help me tolerate this new rule.

Who would be Mecnun[182] in front of Him?
Anyone whose Heart is wounded by His Love
Becomes Leylâ.
The good Leylâ consumes
All the patience and decisions of other Leylâs.

Son, hold your father's hand.
Take care of him until morning,
Because I have been overwhelmed
By the sparks of the cloud
Which rains fire over me.

Since wine is forbidden for him,
The Soul becomes restless.
Once he drinks, the unlucky Saturn
Won't let him see my moon-faced Beauty.

The Soul has been trembling because of Him,
But he deserves all this trembling.
Where are the eyes
That search the waves
Of my endless seas and being
Which are sacrificed in those waves?

O the King of the five senses
And the six dimensions!
I will talk about Him
Until the Last Day of Judgment.
Even amazement is astonished
That I am so close with Him.

Either tell or don't.
I have no patience for that game.
O Beloved whose face is mine this year,
His hair was mine last year.

People are scared of Him.
For me, death is like sugar in His temple.
Life without Him is my death.
Praise without Him is my shame.

O deceiving moon,
O star that doesn't befriend
My leftover knowledge!

My Beautiful, I will turn around this pivot;
I will hide in privacy from the stars.
But where is the morning
Of the Ones who drank the morning wine?
Where is the assembly of free people?

O One who speaks these words,
Be a friend to the wrestler of aged, bored people,
Because these languages, quatrains, poems
Have tired me.

Don't mention anyone except Shems of Tebriz.
Don't say anything
That isn't either help or victory.
Don't talk about anything
But Love and burning Hearts.
I won't acknowledge anything else.

100.

Verse 1266

*Y*ou are just like a Soul inside of my Soul,
Flowing secretly and stealthily.
O light of my garden, my meadow,
You walk and sway like a cypress.

Since you're going, don't go without me.
O Soul of my Soul, don't go without the body.
O gleaming light, don't go away
From my eye. Don't go!

I'll tear the seven layers of sky,
Cross seven seas
If You look charmingly
At my dizzy-headed Soul.

O Beauty whose face is my faith,
Whose looks are my religion,
The believer and disbeliever become my slaves
When You are in my arms.

O Joseph of Canaan, you took my hands, my feet
And made me without hands and feet,
Cut me off from food, drink, sleep,
Came inside drunk and laughing.

I turned into Soul with Your kindness,
I passed out of myself.
O Beautiful whose existence
Has disappared from my eyes
But is hidden within myself!

O Beautiful whose eyes
Make the narcissus drunk!
The rose tears its dress because of You.
Branches are full of buds with Your Grace,
O my endless garden meadow.

One moment You pull me
To the mountain next to the garden.
Another moment, in order to open my eyes,
You lead me to the source of light.

O the Soul who is better than all Souls,
O the mine which is better than
The most valuable mine,
O my most attractive, most charming Beauty!

Since this place is not our country,
Let this flesh be decayed, go to pieces.
I'm not afraid. I don't even think of the sky,
O One whose Union
Is like meeting with Saturn.

The Soul resembles little particles in the air
Without Your sun.
Why does my foundation
Of the four foundations,[183]
My pillar of the four pillars,
Become alone, without You?

O my Sultan Selahaddin,
O One who knows, shows the way,
Doesn't care for my composure,
The One who is above all possibilities!

101.

*H*ow long do you think you can escape death
By watching the purple color of the Judas tree,
By listening to the sound of the organ?
Look and see.
They're pulling and dragging you away.
Really, we are returning to Him.

How long will you lock the houses with greed?
How long will you keep indulging in food,
Chasing the bait?
The trap of death has already exhausted you.

There is no need for a silver saddle
On a dead horse.
When you ride the wooden horse
And use the slab as a saddle,
You'll understand all the deceit and fables of life.

Take off your expensive dresses and skirts;
Surrender yourself to the shroud.
Move away from the greenness, the garden;
Try to stay on the ground with the blood.

You used to watch beautiful ones stealthily,
Used to be their confidant.
You used to come over, clapping your hands.
Where are they now? What happened to them?

You bent your jaw[184] to nice people,
Made fun of them.
Now they've tied your jaw.[185]
Your son, your wife have removed you
From the house.

Where are your night-drinking joys and parties,
Those sugar-tasting lips?
Where is the breath you used
To blow spells up to the moon
With your mind, your talent?

Where is the time when you refused
To give bread to the needy?
Where are your fights,
In which you jumped over crumbs of bread?
O the One who was dumped in the hole
Upside down,
Where is your necklace?
Where are your headbands?

Where is your incongruous,
Nonsensical business?
Where is your annoyance, your discord?
Where is your ambition in work, in deceit?
Your tracks, O imposter?

O the one who says this garden is my garden,
This inn is my inn,
This one is mine, that one is mine!
The one who says "mine" weighs seventy tons.
Now, even a single piece of straw
Is more valuable than you.

Where is that stately pride,
Your sarcastic smile, your dislike of everyone?
Where are those attacks, those fights
In which your face got all red
Because of your crazy anger?

Not even one night did you repent until morning,
You didn't remember God,
Didn't even mention His name.

Today, you'll be beaten and sorry for the past,
Because of your crazy beliefs and loose faith.
You repent for loving the past.

You repent being a stranger to God,
And yet stay away from the prophets.
How does this happen, how?

My friend, be like a mirror,
Tell legends without tongue or lips.
If action gives sadness,
Drunkenness goes away.

102.

I turn so much around my Heart,
That my body cannot carry my weight;
Nor can my Soul stand my fight.

I will turn around this mine
Until my being is totally disintegrated.
My wires will be entirely broken.

Son, you are obstinate. So am I.
Sometimes even the male lion
Bends his head when faced with my persistence.

How can the body
Not turn around the Soul,
Which looks like a sky with torches?
O Beauty! The attraction point
Of my compass-like Soul!

The millstone turns as water comes.
You wouldn't know that.
You said that it's enough
For all my wheat to become flour.

But the millstone doesn't care
For your floor or your grain.
As long as water comes,
It turns around my secrets
Like a whirling sky.

I am a sieve in His hands.
He moves and turns me around.
That is His business.
To be a sieve is my business.

Neither truth nor appearance remain.
Water is gone, grass is gone.
Seizing the moment, I say,
"O my rose-faced Beauty, come."

O One who becomes Soul
To my drunk Soul,
The One who escaped last night from my hand,
Be kind to me. Look at my broken heart.

O my Soul, beg that Beloved
That He calls you thus:
"O my Soul, O my sustenance, my livelihood!"

My body looks like a spindle
When I am in silence.
God, keep spinning my thread,
Make a ball out of the threads of my body.

The thread and spinning of the thread
Are invisible.
The spindle and its turns are visible.
The spindle says, "Without His hold and pull,
How can I do this work?"

The body is like a turban.
The Soul looks like a head.
The body covers the Soul
In every curve like a turban.

O Shemseddin, You are
Sometimes like a turban, sometimes a head.
I'm afraid You'll find an excuse
To change Your mind about meeting me
And disappear.

103.

O my fast, quick flyer,
Fly to the land of Absence;
Don't stay on this side.
Go to the house of secrecy,
O my thought, my understanding.

What else does this world have
But a drum on the feast day
Of this universal intelligence?
In the harvest of my skies,
This sky offers nothing but a piece of straw.

I wounded your Heart,
Don't try to put salve on my wound.
I tore your mantle,
Don't try to grab my torn mantle.

It's better to look at what I do,
Because I am the complete Fountain of Life.
O one who is afraid
That I will destroy him,
Don't carry around that kind of feeling about me.

This sea isn't even a drop
On the coast of the sea of Soul.
Joy isn't even a grain
In my time of sorrow.

Rabbits, pheasant and gazelles
Are hunted by kings.
Look at the male lions
That are tied on my stirrups,
Hanging upside down.

Because of my Beloved,
Who is the Beauty of the land,
"I created the skies because of You." [186]
The Hearts of lions were turned into blood.
The valley was spread with blood.
The One who makes man is Mecnun,[187]
Becomes Mecnun.

If you're tired and bored,
Come, drink a small glass of God's wine,
The wine which moves and shakes man
And makes the mountain of Uhud[188] disappear.

This is the kind of wine
Whose light reflects
The sky which is not supported
By poles and walls.[189]
If you drink a drop of it,
You will understand
All the exuberance of my Soul.

This wine affects your insides,
Sharpens your mind,
Enlightens your eyes, your Heart,
So that in time, you will see
The pearl inside of this flimsy body.

The world is like a chicken
Sitting on an incubating egg.
The arms and wings of my angels
Are nourished by this egg.

One day, the chicken goes away
With the fear of a kick
And leaves the egg alone.
At that time, my seven-level sky disappears
In the light of my clean egg.

The bottomless sea says,
"O old earth, lift up your skirt.
Pick up a pearl from me.
My eyes are not jealous or protective."

I am beyond illusion.
The mind fails to understand me.
The one who can see my peer, my partner,
Is the one who sees double
Because of confusion.

My words are like a toothbrush
Which cleans your teeth,
Makes your mouth beautiful.
Even then, you should be silent,
Because when you're in silence,
You plunge more deeply
Into the world of ecstasy.

104.

Verse 1322
(Same as gazel 101, except these verses)

O One whose perfume fills the air on my way.
O One whose, "Ah," becomes my company.
With the Love of my Beloved Sultan of Sultans,
Color and smell fall in Love with me.

My Soul has ascended to the sky
Like a particle devoid of weights;
So why is the essence of my four pillars,
My foundation,
Without You, separated from You?

105.

My Beloved was walking about
The garden yesterday, saying,
"O greenness, there are hundreds
Who tolerate your oppressions,
But is there anyone like me?"

I asked Him, "Why don't you ask this of me?"
"My questions," He answered,
"Don't fit in the ear
And don't come from the mouth."

"Even if You don't ask me openly,
Tell me secretly," I said.
"The Soul and body both will be burned
By secret explanations, hints
And signs of the Heart," He answered.

"In what manner do you go
On this journey?" I asked.
"Like the moon," He said.
"I go in my orbit, bright, beautiful and playful."

To turn around himself is only for the Pivot.[190]
Because he is on a journey in his country,
He walks while standing.

The caravan master and camels
Are all drunk from the Sultan of Sultans.
O caravan master, don't stay anywhere
Except my Beloved's place.

O our drink, our whims,
O our essence, our beginning!
How does the Soul of Hasan or Abu-l Hasan[191]
Know our secret?

O the One whose Love in my Soul
Resembles the sun in the sign of Aries,
Whose stature, face and eyes
Turn into Yemen's[192] ruby in my eyes!

The ones before, the ones after,
If they all get together
At the end of the world,
None will be more beautiful than You.

If Mecnun[193] sees You, he'll forget Leylâ.
If Leylâ sees you,
She'll get in the same trouble as Mecnun.

The rose has so many thorns in its feet
Just from searching for You.
The jasmine cries all the time
Because of its separation from You.

All the particles in both worlds
Wouldn't greedily open their mouths
If the sun of Your face didn't give us sustenance.

When an animal is sacrificed,
Its soul leaves its body.
Piece by piece, its meat comes back
To life on this side.

Fire teaches eternal living
To those pieces of meat.
"O the one just freed from the Soul,
Who becomes Nothing,
Tries to reach the Soul
Which cannot be damaged."

Those pieces of meat yell, saying,
"I wish my tribe could know
And understand that!"
If those yells ever come this way,
Arrogance and disbelief among the people
Will disappear.

There will be no fear in any Heart,
Nor thorn in the foot of any rose.
You'll march to reach this country, saying,
"I accept Your invitation,
I accept Your invitation!" [194]

There's an end to this longing.
I can tell it if the Cupbearer comes
And makes me go out of myself.

106.

My Beloved, walking
Around the garden yesterday
And talking to the plants, said,
"There are hundreds of people
Who suffer because of you.
But is there anyone like me?"

You didn't appreciate my lips.
You argued with me.
See how much you've wasted me,
Making me admired by the people of our time.

O instigator!
The One who throws fire at the people
Hangs every Heart,
With invisible thread, from the sky.

All this world is like garbage
In Your clean, pure sea.
Only the Souls and Hearts of men and women
Play in Your sea.

You light so many candles
And lamps beyond the sky.
You make so many shapes
Beyond the house of Souls and bodies.

O most Beautiful,
If there isn't an image of Your face,
All of the realities turn into image.
If it isn't You,
The Soul in my body becomes dead,
Wrapped in its shroud.

O my eyes don't see anything
Without His glory.
O my Soul dies without His Soul,
Which adds Soul to Soul.

I said, "Why are you asking
All this from me?"
"Our questions," he said,
"Don't touch ears and mouths."

O the one who thinks
The shadow of the beloved is the Beloved
And doesn't differentiate a shirt from flesh!

When your limited, counted Soul
Merges with limitless, countless Soul,
Your Soul cannot fit in your body.
Your candle cannot be covered.

107.

*Y*ou flee in every direction,
But, no, don't flee from our circle.
Don't run away from our circle.
O moon, you're spoiling
The galaxies of the Pleiades.
No, no. Don't do that.

You are Nev-rûz, [195]
Full of fire, full of light.
We're like the night following you.
Wherever you stay, we go there.
No, no. Don't do that.

O Sun, at the sign of Aries,
Garden and field are dressed
By your kindness, your honor.
Without You, they were idle,
Wounded by winter.
No, no. Don't do that.

O the One whose Sun
Has become a nanny for us,
We're a shadow following You.
O nanny, without Your Grace, we're lonely,
No, no. Don't do that.

108.

*Y*our Love came later,
But surpassed the others,
So much greater than other Loves.
Clearly, God wrote His commandment to say,
"And the last ones went further."[196]

His imperial cipher has inscribed in gold,
"Truly, we did open!"[197]
His form has appeared
Out of the blue color of the Soul's sea.

Adam has come once more
To sit at the throne of religion.
The ones who are identified by
"We stay in line"[198]
Bend their heads gratefully
In an act of prostration.

Who is Rüstem[199] compared to
The line of Lovers in this world,
Lovers riding their black horses
On the sea of blood every day.

Hundreds of bodiless heads are swimming
And saying with smiles,
"Truly we'll return to Him."[200]
They are in the sea of blood
Because of Your clamor and greatness.

When the shadow of the Lover
Falls on the stone mountain,
The mountain jumps to the nine-level sky.
"Really, it's the truth we believe,"
It says a hundred times.
Try it if you don't believe it.

He shines. His light reflects off that mountain.
Listen to all the noises in it.
What is the position of that poor mountain
Compared to Moses who became helpless?

The sky is an ordinary ladder in front of Moses.
Where is the sky? Where is the rope?
Where is the Soul?
Where in this degraded world?

You are the sun, a golden plate.
God boiled your kettle.
God cooked your meal.
Before, you were wanted.
How did you become the one who wants?

He was planted last year.
This year He grew leaves,
Raised them above the ground,
Casting spells on Himself.

The Soul became drunk with the glass He offered.
What a glass, what a cup!
It is such a cup that even the sky
Turned upside down to be prostrate before Him.

O Shems of Tebriz, more beautiful
Than the Garden of Eden,
You played my harp
With your Grace and kindness;
I became an organ in the universe of Love.

109.

Verse 1367

𝒥've seen a thief.
He was stealing people's belongings and money.
But why does our Thief
Steal from that thief?

If a thief becomes too much trouble,
People ask the Sultan for help.
If the Sultan starts stealing,
Where do they go for help then?

Love is the Sultan
Who steals the Heart of all thieves.
In this way, God pulls these rebels,
By seizing their forelock,[201]
To the front of that unruly mob.

Love is the Sultan who steals
All the Shahnes'[202] Hearts,
And at His place,
There are all kinds of Shahnes.

Last night I yelled to the sleeper,
"There's a thief here."
That Thief quickly stole
My tongue from my mouth.

I tried to tie His hands,
But instead He tied mine.
I wanted to lock Him up in prison,
But He can't be contained
In the whole world.

Because of His sweet style of stealing,
The guards become thieves.
The smart ones disappear
Because of His cunning.

I saw a bunch of people
In the middle of the night, asking,
"Where is the Thief?"
He was also asking, "Where is the Thief?"
He was among them,
But nobody could see Him.

O the One who is the source of every word
Appears as an enemy,
Then puts on a friend's face.
O the One who is eternal life
Comes suddenly as a tragedy.

O the One who walks in the Heart's blood,
May the Heart be your lawful right.
Hit and wound me.
I'm not asking for Your mercy.

O the One who stretches the bow,
Shoot that beautiful arrow at me.
I would be sacrificed to Your bow and arrow.

The wound You open in my vessel is life for me.
It adds Soul to my Soul.
Even then, it's a pity
To cut my body,
Which has turned into a reed flute,
In half with Your sword.

Where is Ishmael's[203] neck
That gives thanks to Your knife?
Where is Circis,[204]
Who gives Life every moment
With the wound You open?

Maybe our King, Shems of Tebriz,
Returns from His journey.
There have only been a few like Him among men.
He's gone, disappeared like Semurg.[205]
Not even a trace of His dust appears.

110.

This is the belief of the infidel;
This is the reward of the One
Who patiently waits;
This One is also the life
Which that One laid down on the ground
And found.
What a beautiful helper!
What a beautiful hope!

Hundreds of suns are ashamed
After seeing Your face, Your beauty.
The sun has been harvesting the clusters
At the sign of Sumbule.[206]
You are in business.
The Heart is beating,
Yelling and screaming in the chest,
So that you can see and understand clearly.

From great angels, there are words like
"O cleanest Soul,
God's compassion to the universe"
In every kind of food.

A door is opened to the truths
Which have been imprisoned.
A freshness, a light comes
To the garden of peonies.
News appears about difficult subjects,
Difficult to understand
Before the Last Day of Judgement.

O Heart, set a trap with your eye.
If you don't have an eye, borrow one.
O Soul, call everyone.
Do everything.
Jump, free yourself from this water, this earth.

O Soul, are you lazy?
You are the lion of great battles.
You have to break the lines
And conquer this enforced castle.

Hurry up, O One who Loves
And wants to be Loved.
Hear us praying "You grant our wishes."
If the Beloved is hidden, unseen,
Look carefully here, for Soul is going to Him.

When the talented Soul plunged
Into the sea of blood,
It wondered with whom it was and said,
"I wish my tribe knew." [207]

He said, "I'm a torrent flowing to the sea.
I'm Soul ascending to the sky.
I'm a ruby, reaching to the pearls,
And either I will become a crown
Or a ring's stone."

The one who has reached
This mind, this understanding,
Tastes that sugar which cannot be counted,
Then brings clear water from the stone,
Like Moses.

Since I've become drunk, I'll jump,
Put the saddle on the Heart's horse,
Because I have the desire for the Sultan,
The One who is greater than all the moons.

265

Never mind all these words.
Talking is the curtain in front of meaning.
If you will drink, drink that wine.
If you will select, select that wine.

It is better to be silent
While waiting and watching,
Because there is always grief with words.
The One who helps has come.
The One who helps has come.
O Moslem, ask for help.

Müstef'ilün, Müstef'ilün,[208] O Great One,
O the One who is closer to us than our self,
Closer than the vessel[209] of our Heart,
Either sitting drunk or up walking!

111.

Play, tambourine. Play, tambourine.
You'll reach the kingdom.
O One who is the confidant
Of men and women,
Be brave; don't worry.

Give power, take power.
O One who is involved with trading,
Don't give up, don't give up.
Go to absolute profit.

If you're concerned about losing your honor,
Don't be afraid.
He'll give you hundreds of honors.
Your Soul will come to life and be saved
From the shame of going to the grave,
The shame of needing the grave digger.

You come here today drunk,
Hit the modesty and shame of each other.
Now, O candle of Soul, shine,
Shine and enlighten everywhere.
Save yourself from the shame
Of going under the basin.[210]

I burned that mantle.
I gave up acceptance and denial of the people.
Tell Abu-l Alâ[211] I don't care if he treats me coldly,
If Abu-l Hasan is mad at me.

If you're noble,
Why are you after gain all the time?
This will bring disgrace,
Especially if you expect something
From the beauty of Huten.[212]

Hundreds of Souls are sacrificed
To my Beloved.
My crown, my turban are sacrificed.
If I go to the stockhole of the bath with Him,
Even heaven is jealous of that.

That stockhole turns into a rose garden.
Ashes and dust become iris.
Like the manners of my Beloved,
It changes in such a way
That it's impossible to describe.

I'll obey the order of my Beloved.
I'll be silent.
I'll follow the rhythm of the rope,
And jump like a rope.

112.

I never knew, never thought
That that moon would take the shape of a human
And come to earth
And that His beauty would throw
All the Chinese beauties into the fire.

It never would have come to mind
That that male lion would come from the forest
And cover the Lovers with blood.

I told my Heart,
"Oh, Heart, once more
You're smeared with your own blood."
"Be silent," he said, "silent.
You should come and see His face once."

Shall I talk about His face or His character?
Shall I praise His bangs or His hair,
His drunk eyes, or His cheeks?
Or mention His forehead?

I've been captivated by Him.
I'm drunk with that wine.
I've fallen down to the ground because of Him.
From night until morning I asked God
And yelled to Moslems to come help me.

Where is some paper?
I'll make a painting,
A face as bright as that Beauty
Who resembles the sun.
Then I will set fire to the belongings
Of water and earth, burn them all.

Earth turns its face to the sky
Because of His separation.
But the sky also screams and says,
"I am as you are a hundred times."

Answers come from the secret land
To both of them.
"O Lovers, O unhappy ones,
Look here, right here.
Happiness is to lay an ambush."

The kingdom is everywhere
With the torch of complete visibility
In its hand, guiding Lovers
On the right way.

With this mighty flame,
The secrets of good ones or bad
Come to the surface,
Like the hair inside of milk.
Today is like the day of resurrection.

The one who has fallen in Love
With Our river won't be thirsty.
The door of the treasure won't close
To the one who is looking for treasure.

O garden, you endured and waited,
Then clouds came over you.
O really patient one,
Patience is the key to tightness and distress.

Is this Moon the sun of earth?
Did it come from the sky?
His Love is like Soul.
I should hide Him like a scream.

I should hide so Soul can taste Him alone.
Tercî will grab His ear
And pull Him from behind the curtain.

* * * * * * * *

Mustafâ[213] asked God,
"Why are You disdainful of us?
Tell us, please.
What's all this about people?
What was the purpose of creating them?"

God said, "O Soul of the universe,
I was a hidden treasure.
I wanted this gift of treasure
And the favor to become apparent.[214]

"I created a mirror;
The back is the earth,
The front is the sky.
The back will be even better
If it escapes from hypocrisy and ostentation."

If the grape wants to be wine,
It has to stay in the jar and ferment.
If the back wants to be the front,
It has to be crushed and mended.

How can muddy water be a desirable mirror?
When it gets rid of the mud,
It becomes clear.

My Sultan says to the Soul
Who flew away from the body,
"Come. Since You left the bad ones,
You're my friend now."

It's well known
That with the treatment of the alchemist,
Copper becomes gold.
The secret Chemist turns copper into gold.

This sun is rich because of God;
It doesn't need a crown or robe.
It has become a hat for hundreds of bald ones
And clothes for all the naked ones.

Jesus rode a donkey
Because of His humility.
If that weren't the case,
How could the morning breeze
Ride a donkey?

You should yell, saying,
"O Soul, make your head
Food on the search.
O mind, be eternal for this eternity!"

Remember God so much
That you forget yourself.
While you're praying
You'll bend like the *dal*[215]
Of the word of praying.

As you know, the bazaar of desires
Is full of deceit and cheating.
O good man, put your mind into your head.
Don't get involved with those useless things.

If you want to reach Soul,
The smiling Kingdom,
Smile like a rose in disfavor
As well as in favor.

O the Soul gives life to every corpse.
This ready meal is carried away
And becomes more and more.
But the third Tercî is coming.

* * * * * * *

If my Cupbearer were here,
I would drink the wine offered to me.
I would learn how to cast
A permanent spell from His magician eyes.

If my cowardly Heart would turn brave
And become His lion hunter,
I would catch one male lion now
And put a saddle on it.

I would be freed from the oxen of body[216]
And ascend to the sky
With the help of hyacinth-like eyebrows[217]
And beautiful harvest moons.

I would leave the assembly of my Sultan
As a drunk,
Rule every town I visit,
Be the cure for every trouble.

I would neither harvest nor sow.
I would become absolute reflection.
I would be neither wet nor dry,
Neither hot nor cold.

I wouldn't get involved with daily bread
Or the trouble of life.
Neither would I roll over the earth, like a ball,
Nor fly to the sky, like dust.

I would turn into neither a dizzy cypress
Nor a dancing hyacinth,
Neither a ruby-dressed tulip, nor yellow saffron.

I wouldn't close my mouth, like a bud
Because of the secret ailment of my Heart.
I would give up this and the other world,
Be nourished by the Glory of God.

The Sultan of Faith says, "Yes, every moment
You have gone through all
And a hundred times more,
Because I was on your track
Saying, 'open the door.'
I was the one sending you
From one situation to the other.

"I am helping the earth, like rain helps greeness!
I am the pair of everyone,
But I am exempt from every pair.
I am the One.

"When Solomon lost his throne,
He started selling fish.
If he had stayed out of trouble,
Why would I hurt him?
I wouldn't even hurt an ant.

"Thorns wouldn't get into the foot of the rose
If there were a summer without winter.
I wouldn't crush the grape
If there were wine without a hangover."

If that witch-woman's knot were untied
From the feet of my Soul,
I would be hundreds of Rüstems,[218]
Hundreds of brave ones,
In spite of the harm
Of the blind hold of man.

Our eyes are bright because of You.
Your life would be eternal, O our joy.
O generous One,
O Charmer who understands us,
My life and hundreds like mine
Would be sacrified to You.

113.

O Lovers, O Lovers,
The One who sees His face
Loses his mind, becomes crazy,
Insane, spread around.
His manners change.

Start looking for the Beloved.
His store is demolished,
Runs face down like water in the river,
Makes His feet His head.

When He becomes Mecnun [219]
In the world of Love,
He starts turning like a universe.
But the ones who are afflicted with this ailment,
In the end, they find His remedy and are cured.

The angel would prostrate
To the one who becomes black dirt for God.
The sky would be a slave and servant
To the one who is a black slave to Him.

His Love picks up the wounded Heart in His hand
And keeps smelling it.
How can the Heart
That's picked up and smelled by Him
Not be good?

He has wounded so many Hearts,
Made so many lose sleep.
This magician's narcissus eyes
Have tied the hands of so many magicians.

All the kings are His poor ones.
All the beauties gather His favor.
Lions are tamed and sit on their tails
In front of His neighborhood dogs.

Look at the sky.
Look at the castle of angels.
On its tower and sides
There are so many torches and lights.

The warden of the castle
Of that Sultan who is without drums
Is the universal intelligence.
Whomever He sees at the castle
Grows and matures.

O moon, have you seen Him?
Did you get this beauty from Him?
O night, have you seen His lovelock?
No, no, no. The most you have seen
Is maybe one lock of His hair.

Tonight is dressed in black.
It must be in mourning.
It's dressed in black,
Like a widow whose husband has died.

Don't believe the night is dying.
It secretly drinks with Him.
It doesn't have eyes,
But sees His eyes and makes Him frown.

O night, I don't ask your help
For my yelling and screaming.
You're also rolled like His ball
With the club of fate.

The One who becomes a ball for His club
Acquires the ball of happiness.
In front of His club,
Like a ball without head and feet,
It keeps running like the Heart.

O our face is saffron-colored
Because of His tulip-red features.
O the Heart is plunged into grief,
Like a comb inside of His hair.

Trust Love. Love is completely
A face and eyes turned this way, watching you.
There is nothing next to Love
Except face and vision.

He doesn't have shape,
But all His work is to make shapes and forms.
O Heart, you cannot do without forms and shapes,
Because you are not from the same origin.

Anyone who has a clean Heart
Will be able to differentiate
The sound of the Heart
From the sound of the body.
This voice is His lion's,
Roaring in the shape of a gazelle.

The things which are woven
By God's hands
Still come from the weaver's hand,
The weaver's shuttle.

O Beautiful One,
Who is the shuttle of the Soul,
O the One
Whose face is the direction in which we pray,
The sky is the one
Who creates and decorates this place.
Earth is his wife.

My Heart has been burning
Because of my jealousy of Him.
My eyes turn into a leather bottle.
But how can I get Him wet?
Even the ocean comes only to His heel.

This Love has become a guest to me;
It hits and hurts my Soul.
This is a reward, a favor for me.
Hundreds of thanks to His arms, His hands!

I gave up my hands, my feet
And quit searching.
O the Friend who wipes out our search
With His searching!

How long will I say, "O Heart, O Heart?"
Give up the Love of Heart. Be silent.
When Heart hears His voice saying, "Hu," [220]
There'll be no use for my worries and troubles.

114.

In the morning before the sun rises,
Light sparkles on the glass dome of the sky.
At night, the blood-red glass of the west
Comes from Your blood-stained arrow's head.

Waters cascade from the canyons.
Torrents eventually reach the coast of Your sea
And merge, mixing with the sea.

With all its height, even the moon
Raises its head to see You,
Dropping its hat to the ground.

In the early dawn the nightingale
Sings songs in Your garden
To the tunes of the ones who have reached You.
They scream like Lovers.

O Beautiful! Souls search for Your face,
For all the Hearts, for the Beloved!
O Charmer, whose big garden
Carries the four overflowing rivers![221]

In one river water runs through.
Another is the river of honey.
See the next one?
It's the river of fresh milk.
The last one is Your river of red wine.

When will You give me a break?
When will You fill me up with wine,
Giving me jar after jar?
How can I tell the mind
The things that this wine does?

Who am I?
Even the sky keeps turning,
Drunk from this great big jar.
He can't be away one moment from Your Love.
For even one moment,
He can't be out of this wine.

O silver-belted moon,
You have known Love for a long time.
O sky, it's obvious from your face
That you are a Lover.

Love which has been a friend to the Heart
Is tired out by the words of the Heart.
Be silent, O Heart.
How long will You be working, searching?

Heart answered me, "I am His reed flute,
I cry with His breath."
I said, "Cry, O One
To whom my Soul will be sacrificed
For His Love."

Really, we opened your door.
Don't separate from your friends.
Thank God for the Love
Which totally covers and holds you.

115.

The tactless one
Who has been jealous and frustrated
Because of Jesus
Should die.
Hundreds of dogs should soil his beard.[222]

How can a donkey hunt gazelle?
How can a donkey
Give off the gazelle's smell of musk?
Who smells the urine of the donkey?
Who looks for the smell of it?

It doesn't hurt running water
If the bitch donkey urinates in it.
But even that one should not drink that water.
It's better to stay thirsty.

O the One whose coquetry and coyness
Are worse than a deviate's,
Whose face-scratchings look like a prostitute's.
Because of such deceit, such cheating,
Even animals become ashamed.
Hear from God,
"They are more deviate than animals." [223]

I'll be silent.
God will make him ashamed for eternity.
I will go to the Cupbearer.
I am drunk from His manners, His humors.

116.

O Love, are You taller and better
Than the apple trees in Your orchard?
O new moon, offer new life to Your admirer.

Bitter becomes sweet if it comes from You.
Blasphemy and deviation turn into religion.
Your pieces and bits become August's rose.
Hundreds of Souls will be sacrificed to Your Soul.

O the One who makes people's heads dizzy,
Put up a ladder to the sky.
Give wings to the men,
Involve them in hundreds of fights.

What a beautiful disposition you have, O Love.
What a beautiful face you have, O Love.
You like so much drinking, O Love,
O One who gives joy to His friends.

It is Your color in the best peony.
Every truth becomes confused in front of You.
Every particle, expecting kindness and generosity,
Turns to You.

Without You, all the bazaars are ruined and lost.
The garden expects Your rain.
So does the orchard, grape and flower.

The trees learn to move from You.
The fresh leaves step on the ground with You.
The leaves and fruits all become drunk
After drinking Your Fountain-of-Life's water.

The garden wants an autumnless spring
As a gift from You,
Because it wants to spread its hair
With Your rose-perfumed winds.

Your shining star brightens the star of Saturn,
Then feels shame on seeing the darkness
Of all these stationary and moving stars.

You have such nice invitations
In Your garden of joys.
The Soul who becomes your guest
Eats joy instead of bread.

I have it tried once;
I cannot find pleasure without You.
How can I find a taste for life
Without Your endless salt?

I went on a journey, came back.
I reached the end, started all over again.
This elephant of Soul[224]
Saw Your India in its dream.

Your India is a square for Your drunks.
Even virgins are pregnant
Because of the pleasure of Your melodies.

I took measures, but they didn't help.
The Heart broke its chains
And dragged the Soul
In front of Your imperial tent.

There, I didn't see any obstinate or cold people.
There was a new life every moment
There were new, abundant favors.

The mountain looks at Your gentleness
And is ashamed.
The Heart becomes insolent
And wants like crazy to jump to Your tent.

You've opened so many doors in iron, in stone,
That Heart turns into an ant
Looking for a crack in Your bowl, Your glass.

I'm incapable of describing You,
To the Last Day of Judgement.
How Your endless sea would be depleted
If I took a glass of water!

117.

Wake up! Wake up! Night is over.
Be disgusted. Be disgusted even with yourself.

Right now, an idiot is selling
Joseph in Egypt.
If you don't believe me,
The bazaar is right here.
Go and see for yourself.

Totally Absolute God
Would devoid you of conditions,
Give you that rose face.
Take the thorns out of your feet,
Then go to the rose garden.

Don't listen to every trick, every deceit.
Why are you washing blood with blood?
Stay upside down like a glass
So that you can drink the wine with sediment.

For His club, be like a ball.
As an appetizer for His vultures,
Be like a carcass.

A voice is heard from the sky, saying,
"The Doctor of Love has come.
If you want Him to come to your side
Become ill, become ill."

Assume His Heart is a cave,
A place of union for the Beloved.
If you are the cave's friend,
Come to the cave, come to the cave.

You are a nice, naive, gullible man.
You lost your gold to thieves.
If you want to know the thief
And get your money back,
Be a pickpocket, be a pickpocket.

Be silent. Don't try to describe
The sea and the pearl in His ocean.
If you want to be a diver,
Hold your breath, hold your breath.

118.

Give up cheating, O Lover.
Be ruined, ruined.
Jump right in the middle of the fire,
Get inside Heart. Be a moth.

Be a stranger to yourself.
Come. After you give up your house,
Stay at the same place,
The same house with Lovers.

Go wash your Heart clean of hate
Seven times, like trays, then come.
Be a glass for the wine of Love.

In order to deserve the Beloved,
Be pure Soul.
If you go to the drunks, be drunk, drunk.

You are the night of Kadir.[225]
Be the night of Kadir here.
Be a palace to the Souls,
Like the night of Kadir.

Wherever your thought goes,
It drags you behind, pulls you there.
Give up thought
So that you may walk in front
Like fate and destiny.

Fancies and pleasures are like a lock
Which closes our Heart.
Be a key.
Be a thread of the key, thread of the key.

You are not lower than the Pole of Hannane,[226]
Which the prophet Muhammed caressed.
Be the Pole of Hannane, Pole of Hannane.

Solomon tells you,
"Hear, learn the language of the birds,"
Yet you have become a trap.
The bird escapes from you.
Don't be a trap.
Be the nest, be the nest.

If Beauty shows His face,
Fill yourself with Him, like a mirror.
If that Beauty opens, spreads His hair
In front of you,
Be a comb, be a comb.

How long will you be running
With two feet like a Ruh,[227]
One foot like a pawn,
Or crisscrossing like a queen?
Put your mind in your head. Be wise.

For gifts and possession
You give Love as gratitude.
Never mind possession and gifts,
Give yourself to Love as gratitude.

For some time you were fire,
Then became wind, turned into water,
Became earth.
For some time you became an animal,
Stayed around in the animal kingdom.
Since you are now Soul,
Try to be a Soul who deserves the Beloved,
A Soul who deserves the Beloved.

O with the ability to talk,
How long will you stay at the roof, at the door?
Go into the house. Quit using words.
Quit talking. Be silent!

119.

Cupbearer, if You haven't had much wine,
Pawn our cup.
As long as this wine
Comes from Your kindness, Your favor,
I would never hesitate to pawn my Soul.

So many eunuchs, so many lords
Have pawned their belongings in our town,
With the drunkeness of God's wine.

Look at Ibrahim Edhem,[228]
Who is riding the horse of knowledge.
That king gave up his throne, his crown.

If that unique, peerless Beauty
Were to drop a little sip of that wine
Into the foundation of that idol,
The infidel would pawn his faith
For the Love of the black stone.

I'm the drunk of that tavern.
I haven't pawned my wings
To just any trap, like a bird.
I've been trapped
Only by a grain of that pearl, only that pearl.

Since you've put your belongings in pawn,
Why are you trembling?
Give up your life for Him.
It's nothing to pawn your Soul for Him.
I wish I had a hundred Souls.
I would pawn them all.

Abu-Bekr[229] pawned his head;
Omer, his son; Osman, his lung.
Abû-Hurayra put up his leather bag
As pawn for Him.

If He treats kings in that way,
Why do you wonder
When the poor pawn all the people for wine?

Be silent. Don't act
Like the nightingale in the rose garden.
The nightingale pawns its head and wings
For this smiling rose.

120.

Jf you see a drunk who knows the secret,
For sure, he is His drunk.
If you see one whose Heart is alive,
For sure, He is the One
Who made him like that.

If you see a head full of joy and music,
Who can't differentiate day from night,
For sure, He is the One who scratches that head.

Everyone on this earth is against each other,
Thirsty for each other's blood.
They're all full of malice, looking for fights,
But this is impossible to talk about
Because of the majestic ties
He has put on our feet.

The one who is offered wine every moment
Grows like a tree.
The devil and also the fairy
Admire his jump and growth.

When you see someone like a lion,
Twirl your mustache slightly.
But if he is fat and ugly
That's what you deserve.
You should see the ones who deserve Him.

Particles are molded
To form your shape with His favor
So that your condition functions
Together with His favor.

What a beautiful valley
Is that valley where only Love walks,
Slowly and gracefully.
There is nothing but God above this valley
And nothing but Absence underneath.

Knitted loosely, the word's fishing line
Is not catching anything anyway.
Knitted loosely, the line will catch only prey
That are also drunk with His line and net.

121. [230]

Verse 1545

𝔍t's impossible to have
A Moon like that in the world.
Concede it, concede, O Heart.
You're threatening me with a fight.
Let's fight.

We are God's drunks,
Drunk from that eternal wine.
You are smart and skillful.
Go and stay where there are names and games.

We dressed in paper clothes[231]
And went to see the King.
You're in love with appearances,
Stay with colorful pencils.

Give your life with the Beloved's love.
A knot cannot be untied without Love.
O Soul, become drunk here,
O mind, become lame here.

Rum[232]saw Your face and became drunk.
Zenci[233] saw Your hair and was ruined.
Either go to the land of Rum or Zenci.

You have fallen into His buttermilk.
As a matter of fact, you were born from His Love.
Even if you run hundreds of miles,
You cannot get away from that idol.

If you are a believer,
He is searching for you.
If you are a disbeliever,
He is calling you.
Walk this way, become faithful,
Go there, become unfaithful.
Both are the same to Him.

Your eye is still in His garden.
Your ear is still in His sweet talk.
Plunge into His wealth, become a bee.
Grab His date branch, grow, spread.

Sky is a bow to His arrow.
Water is under His command.
If you are straight, be like an arrow.
If you are crooked, turn into a crab.

He has an endless, big, beautiful country.
Whatever or whomever you are,
You are needed there.
Become an agate, ruby, brick or stone.
All are necessary in that country.

Ruby or stone, come.
Fall into this torrent of trouble.
Go to the sea with the torrent.
Be the guest for that lively Love.

That sea resembles Hizir's[234] Fountain of Life.
No matter how much you drink
It doesn't decrease.
If it does, you feel bad
In your Heart and Soul.

Swim like a fish in the sea.
When you remember dryness,
Go toward the land.

Sometimes He puts His lips to yours;
Other times He puts you on His lap.
First be a reed flute;
Then become a harp.

He has no enemy. His drunks are all around.
Don't stay in the land of solitude.
The day of parade has come for Lovers.
Walk in the front. Be a leader.

Whoever is unaware of His vineyard
Is needy for wine.
It's a vineyard full of wine and grapes.
Sometimes it becomes wine; other times, opium.

Be silent like Mary.
Let the One who has Jesus' breath talk.
Who told you to be a friend
Of the donkey between jobs?

122.

I swear to God, I'm tired
Of glass, earthen and wooden jars.
Where is the Cupbearer
With a Heart as large as the sea
Who offers me the pitcher like a glass?

Offer me the one
To which I'm accustomed.
Don't hide surreptitiously from me.
You have it. Don't search here and there.

You've fooled me every time, saying,
"Why don't you come to Our gathering?"
You say, "Whatever you want,
Come and whisper it in my ear."

Well, I swallowed Your lie.
I didn't look, I didn't think.
Since I'm like a doorbell on the outside,
How can I place my lips to your ear,
Say anything to You?

I'm at the door you've already reached.
My Soul is like foam.
Your Heart like the sea.
For God's sake, quit being lazy.
Pour wine as though You're shedding
My enemy's blood.

As long as mind is my friend,
There is no essence to my words.
Every moment, an image comes
And puts its head on the ground in His temple.

My God, day is added to his day
By the one whose face becomes rose-red
With Your wine,
Because he becomes Hizir [235]
And, like Hizer,
He performs ritual ablutions
With the Fountain of Life.

A voice came from the sky and said,
"We are all to be sacrified to your assembly.
How lucky for friends, how lucky!
Be happy with these favors.
Keep drinking."

The gathering that drinks this wine
Has become cheerful,
With glasses here, glasses there.
In the end, their insides
Have turned into bazaars.

Everyone has passed out.
No one is aware of himself.
Everyone has closed the door, loosened his belt.
Oh son, we are gone. Wash your hands of us.

I am drunk with Your lively eyes,
The tuft of Your hair.
I am saved from color and smell
Because of that rose-colored wine.

Be silent. Don't make the sounds
Of noise and confusion.
Neither noise nor confusion fit here
With the Grace of God.

I was out of myself last night until dawn.
My mind was out of my head.
For one moment, where was the beginning?
Where was the end?

O Shems of Tebriz,
O the one Heart and Soul that became a slave!
Although You wrote my name on the river,
Maybe You've forgotten me.
Even so, come back, come.

123.

Ⓞ One who has good intentions,
Start the journey.
Find the one who can direct you the right way,
Seek the roads.
To reach Him, search everywhere.
The One who will give you happiness,
Where is that great One?
How can you find Him?

Love is a light, exalted,
A secret river to be drunk,
Purified and flowing forever,
A fire burning, never extinguished.

Love goes together with suffering,
But it is the greatest.
If they say the one who Loves can fly,
It's true. Don't deny it.

It's better to be a slave
And serve Him with pleasure,
Than to be a free wanderer.
The one who cries with Love
Doesn't have an eye ache;
His eyes are not sick.

No one knows a Lover's business.
There is no cure for his illness.
Suffering is the best cure for him.
Don't think too much about anyone
Who hasn't fallen in Love,
Hasn't stayed in the valley of Love.

Friends, don't be discouraged.
Compassion comes after trouble.
Don't put on any dress but Love.
Don't cover yourself with any garment but Love.

Knots have been tied
On the strings of Love's spell.
The pain and suffering of Love's fire
Is all ablaze.
Love is such a lost blessing
That anyone who doesn't try to find it
Is deprived.

The day I met my Beloved,
I screamed, I lost my mind.
My trials to avoid guilt all disappeared.
But this is Absence inside of Presence.
This is eternal blessing.

If Love slips out of your hand
Don't fall into despair. Keep searching.
Fight to find it.
Until you reach Him, see Him,
Don't sleep, don't eat, don't relax.

124.

O Lovers, O Lovers, I'm crazy, insane.
Where is the chain?
O One who rattles the chain of Soul,
The world is filled with these rattles and jingles
Because of You.

You made another chain
And hung it around my neck.
To stage a hold-up of the caravan,
You ride a horse from the sky.

Get up, O Soul, free yourself
From the land of soil. Ascend.
That torch in the sky
Is turning around just for us.

How could rain stop the journey
Of one who has grief in his Heart?
How could the mud slow him?
He halts only for Love.
No other place is for him.

A coward yelled one day.
"Bad shepherd," he said,
"That goat in the herd looks at me.
Do you think it will bite me?"

The shepherd answered the coward,
"Even if it bites you
Or kills you under its feet,
The brave one wouldn't mind,
Wouldn't be afraid of the goat."
The coward said, "You're right."

Where is the mind that lets you talk?
Where are the legs that let you
Run from the land, jump in the sea,
Be safe from earthquakes?

You'll be the Sultan of Sultans.
Your sovereignty will be permanent.
Your place will be higher than Saturn.
You'll be free from this rubbish heap.

You'll do the business of universal intelligence,
Be exuberant and overflowing
Like a river of honey.
You'll be the sun at the sign of Hamel, [236]
The moon at the sign of Sünbüle. [237]

A hundred ravens, a hundred owls
And a hundred doves will make tunes for you.
If you give up loitering,
You'll hear the secrets of the Heart.

If you have Heart, fall in Love.
Lose your Heart.
If you have mind, be crazy,
Because this individual mind
Looks like a drop of water
To the eyes of Love.

In the end, Absence comes
And pulls you out of this world of appearances.
Things have become confused
Because of his curly black hair;
It doesn't straighten easily.

But even so, you're to raise up your skirt nicely
On that road
Because there is so much Lovers' blood there.

Go, O Heart, go with the caravan.
Don't try to walk alone,
Because this pregnant time
Gives birth to many troubles.

If you go the way I've told you,
You'll have no trouble.
Your journey will be
With the Mercy of God.
You'll sail like a ship on the sea.
O Heart, since you're going,
You may as well go the easy way.

If you take your Heart away from your Soul,
You'll be saved from war and peace.
You'll need neither the store nor provisions.

Your Soul will be separated from thoughts.
The road to danger will be closed.
Your desire will reach you
And be friendly with you.

You're saved during the day
From that troublemaker from the land of Rum.
Don't be afraid
When the black of night comes with bells.

Be silent, O sweet face.
Go, water carrier,
Tie the head of the water sack,
Because waves cannot be contained
By jars and glasses.

125.

Ⓞ Beautiful, whose Love
Makes the Archangel Gabriel dance in the sky
And the stars and universe
Become exuberant and overflow!

Under the sky, everything
From the oxen to fish is cheerful.
Everything above the sky
From the sign of Taurus
To the sign of Pisces is dancing.

The Lover whose Heart is full of blood
Has gone to the tavern,
Has put such a fire into the wine
And started playing inside the jar.

Heart has seen that honor and respect
Have been poured on His soil
And has started playing with fire, with difficulty.

Souls, like the Prophet Job's,
With the joy of Your kindness, Your favor,
Are dancing in troubles,
Their bodies full of worms.

The Souls of generations
Coming from the family of Adam
Are dancing in Your land of Absence.

The Sultan of Sultans goes on dancing
Without the robe of honor
In the tavern of Absence,
Then becomes Hakan [238]
Without throne and crown.

A group of people have seen
Just a little bit of something,
But they've ended up with greed.
Because of honor and pride
They started dancing alone,
Without being seen by others.

The ones who are full of pride and self
Cannot deserve to be Sultan.
Greatness and exaltation keep dancing
Because of the greatness of that Sultan.

One group of people plays for bread and soup;
The other falls in Love.
They don't care; they just keep dancing.

How nice for that pearl
That it plunged into His sea.
In the end, He Himself turned into a choice sea,
Dancing with that choice.

Where is the one
Who tries to imitate with his mind,
Then turns with fear, acquires hope,
And starts dancing with that hope?

Even then, this one is better
Than the one who denies or is heedless.
At least, time by time, he conforms
And is relieved from the world
Of is not,
Then starts dancing.

There are some who've given up
Existence as well as non-existence
With His Love.
Still others, with His Love,
Say, "I am annihilated and keep dancing."

Bats in the dark are dancing
With the Love of darkness.
The birds which Love the sun
Dance from dawn to sunset.

O fast-blowing morning breeze,
Go and tell Shems of Tebriz,
"Tell me about Yourself.
Come and dance with me."

126.

*L*ook at the drunks.
They've all gathered around our drunk,
Left their minds, thoughts and health.
They've all gotten into trouble.

I told them, "O Soul's drunks,
"O ones who drink wine from the hand of Soul,
Hundreds of thousand of Hearts and Souls
Come close to you, holding you."

They answered, "Thanks to God!
With His Grace, that moon has risen.
We were stuck with deprivation
At the bottom of poverty.

"We escaped from His cruelty,
Stayed away from Him for awhile.
We were like an enemy
And suffered torture and cruelty.

"We put aside the glass of loyalty,
Left work and business,
Gave up the profitable, but tasteless stores."

The mind which puts salve in its eyes
Knows everything
And becomes the friend
Of the ones who have beautiful eyes,
Then starts hanging around with them.
The raven spies upon and lands
Where there's a hanging corpse.

If you have taste in your mouth
You can taste His sweet, bitter jars.
Is it better to give up pleasure and fancies,
Or get hung up on them?

My Heart has been like a vagabond all my life
Because of His Love, looking for Him.
Once I looked, I saw that poor Heart
Has been glued to God.

O brave one, if you trust this house of earth,
I will show you the One who hangs you,
Chains you in, then sets you free.

See the ones who have been murdered
In the land of eternity,
But whose Souls are alive?
They are hung on the gallows of consent,
Like young Mansür.[239]

O Love, You are my Sultan.
Set gallows for me.
The lamp which isn't suspended
Doesn't illuminate the house.

I'm the ground for the feet of the person
Who is attached to the brave One.
I'm a slave and servant to the copper
Which is attracted by secret chemistry.

Get up, jump, tune the instrument,
Start the pleasure, Sema.
It isn't nice for the reed flute
To stay without a melody
Or the tambourine to hang on the wall.

The tambourine unties the Heart;
The reed flute gives new Soul to the ill.
How can the Soul-giver stay closed,
The Heart-opener stay hung?

Today, try to be generous.
Give your Heart.
Haten[240] was saved from being a disbeliever
Because of his generosity.

Generosity is like a trap for bread,
But cleanliness and joy are the trap for the Soul.
Where is the One who holds generosity?
Where is the Other
Who brings our joy and cleanliness?

Generous is the one who gives all his possessions
In the cave with fear.
Sufi, on the other hand, is like Abû-Bakr [241]
Who was held by Muhammed in his arms.

This one fell in Love with a Beauty,
Sacrificed his life to Hakan.[242]
The one who is after advantage
Is hindered by money and goods
And keeps bargaining like a customer.

This One is like a shark
Which plunged into the sea;
The sea admires him.
The other is like a novice swimmer,
Looking for someone to hold.

All these jobs, this work,
This noise and clamour are real or show.
But at the place where we are with Lovers,
Real and show become the same truth.

Night comes, O my dear Soul,
O the eye and light
Of the One who travels at night.
O Charmer who resembles the moon,
For You the moon has been suspended in the sky
Because of its admiration.

I'm as cheerful as the new moon.
You're adding Soul to Soul
Like a new position, a new kingdom.
O Beautiful, whose grief
Bends the new moon down, like me!

Soul is like a great mountain with its knowledge.
Flesh is like a piece of straw.
Who has ever seen a piece of straw
Elevate the mountain?

You've left the one who's been on the road.
Don't get involved with strangers.
You'll get in trouble.
You'll turn into the one
Who's hoping to get help from troubled ones.

Even the Soul of the great One
Turned into blood by thinking
Of the end of the road.
The ones who are assumed to be bad,
Their souls were hanging upside down.

Clean Souls of great men gave up
Thinking of the end,
After seeing what seed the Soul has sown,
And turned back to the beginning.

Heart is the one who calls.
The sound of Heart echoes
On the mountain of body.
O the one who hangs on sound,
Be silent.
Instead, embrace the place
From whence sound comes.

The words coming from the mouth
Give contempt.
Finish your pleading.
Leave contempt. Grab the wisdom of greatness.

127.

Verse 1648

Who is that? Who is that?
He came nicely as a drunk,
Put his shoes under his arms
And walked slowly into our house.

He admires him.
The head of thoughts is dizzy.
Hundreds of minds and Souls
Are handless and footless in front of him.

That ruby-lipped Beauty played a trick
And came with a shovel in his hand,
Asking for fire.
I wonder what the purpose was
Of his coming alone like that.
Who was he going to burn?

O source of the fire, come.
Why do you ask fire from us?
O Beloved, with your untimely arrival,
I swear to God, this is a trick;
This is a spell.

O his face is as bright as the morning sun!
O corner of the house
Which has become a plain, a valley
From the glory of his face,
How could the veil hide you?

O Joseph over the well,
Your reflection shines on the well's water.
That water boils, overflows
From the light of your face.

Welcome, welcome!
You are even a teacher to magicians.
You came from the assembly of the phoenix
Like the Prophet's bird of hoopoe.

O one who is the Fountain of Life
In my lungs,
Every one of your tortures is sweeter
Than ten tons of sugar.
You appear in a different form every moment
From great God.

O Heart-catching Beauty,
You can't fit any angle.
O Beloved, I shed more tears than the oceans
For your beauty.

Earth and sky are a mirror
To your Moon face.
That mirror came to life,
Started watching you.

My God, save me from science, from deeds
Before my last day,
Especially from the words
That come out of the mouth.
Save me from the science of language itself.

O Love's longing has penetrated my mind!
O Beloved! Be silent, be silent.
Hear me telling things
In a different way from now on.

128.

Who is this? Who is this
Who has come suddenly into our circle?
He is the Glory of God. He has come from God.

See this favor, this kindness?
Watch this fortune, this kingdom.
He came like the moon to help the unlucky ones.

Look at the beautiful Leylâ,[243]
How much she desires Mecnun.
Look at the amber of Soul,
Come just to attract the grasses to itself.

Souls come to the door
Because of the taste of His perfumes, His beauty,
His beautiful manners, His saying, "Come."[244]

He draws hundreds of pictures
Of men and the Sultan who has the flag
To Absence.
He paints many different paintings.
All these images please the Heart.

That Beauty who needs nothing
Gives life to these images.
These last forms come to life one by one.

Ascend from this bitter water's well
By hanging on the bucket of the Koran.
O Joseph, this bucket
Was sent to the bottom just for you.

O words, when I give you up,
Then I will reach
The shade of the Sultan
With the sun of knowledge.

My God, save me from science, from deeds
Before my last day,
Especially the talk and words
Which come from my mouth.
Save me from them.

129.

Soil becomes body with Your favor.
From talk and thought,
So many forms and shapes
Become pregnant in the land of Absence.

You feed growth in every form and shape,
But there is meaning, which You freeze.
Shapes and forms are the source of it.

The one who doesn't know the origin of ice
Will know it without doubt
Once he sees ice become water.

Don't think anything but good things,
Because thoughts are the strings
Of the fabric of shapes.
Good thoughts make the best shapes.

They come the way you look at them.
Forms are structured by way of look,
Then they are dressed as men and women.

Stay with the enlightened One,
Because a window is open for Him in the Heart.
Earth grows roses and irises,
But water becomes land for them.

If you associate with God,
You become a beautiful, unconditional Soul,
And so bright, O my God.
O the One who becomes Soul to my Soul!

A kingdom, a glory has come from somewhere.
The time for sorrow is gone.
Now is the time for joy.
A halo has surrounded
The full moon without hands and feet.

How can I see the One
To whom my Soul, my faith
Has become a slave, a servant?
O my God, where is my dignity
In front of Him?
He is the One who gives composure to my mind.

He is the confidant of every particle,
Company for every breath.
The one who doesn't see
Becomes devout because of Him.
The One who sees
Becomes unconventional because of Him
And doesn't care for anything.

O the One whose passion becomes God's Love,
The One who searches in the searcher,
The One who blows His own reed,
The One who wants mine!

He is the One who desires to be desired,
The One who Loves and is Loved.
He is Joseph. He is Jacob.
He is the necklace. He is the neck.

Cut short the descriptions.
Don't search too much.
He doesn't have an end like you.
How long will I play with water and oil,
Pass time with the impossible?
However, my water and oil are both gone.
I have attained my desire.

130.

O Beautiful!
Heart and Soul have fallen in Love
And keep dancing at Your assembly.
O the One!
Innumerable heads have been cut
And dropped to the ground in Your battle.

O Archangel Gabriel!
Once you desired to come to this earth,
All the particles on the ground heard;
They all started dancing.

When your timely order came that
"The blood of the Heart should be shed,"
O my Sultan, blood put on make-up
To beautify other blood.
Appreciate that order. Start dancing.

O One who is most capable
Among all the Sultans, from the Prophet to Adam,
Pawn my Soul. He is in the game
Because he heard Your desire.

Kharezms[245] have denied
God's absolute countenance,
But because of Your sight,
They start dancing by tapping their feet.

O the Sun of His face routed the moon,
Which is happy with Your embrace.
Start dancing.

If Shems of Tebriz
Looks at the Koran of the Heart just once,
That Koran's learning lines
Will start dancing with Your desire.

131.

On this side, there are a few uncovential ones
Hidden in His shadow.
That Sun, through the roof of Heart,
Reflects and shines in their Heart.

Every star turns into Venus.
Every particle becomes the sun.
The sun and stars change into particles
In front of them.
They keep whirling.

Every one of them who's lost his mind
Ascends seven layers of sky,
Where the star of Saturn is, like Keyhusrev,[246]
Without a tent and flag, a Sultan.

You've been on a ride a long time,
Turned around the world.
This time, journey to the land of Soul;
See the tribe of Souls.

Even with God's favors,
God's Beauty, God's grace,
Still, they are overwhelmed by command
And stay under orders.

Their Hearts are like a mirror
Without dirt or rust.
Their Hearts have become square like the sky,
And the Sultan has landed on the square.

Snakes and sugar have
Become cheaper in our town
Because of their sweet yells and ruby lips.

If I were in ecstasy like I was last night,
If it wouldn't worry the instigator,
I would tell the rest of it,
Being out of myself.

But I close my mouth
Because I'm by myself now.
I'll keep silent until my Heart
Becomes drunk with that wine.

O the Sultan of Soul,
God's Shems of Tebriz,
Every Soul becomes a sea because of Him,
Every body turns into coral.

132.

Ⓞ One who is tired
Of me and my work,
I become more thirsty every moment.
What do You lose
If You grant one of my wishes?

If Absence becomes apparent
Because of You,
If Non-existence finds a dress, puts it on
And has one flag from existence,
What do You lose?

It would reach the level
Which deserves Your pity,
Where it reads a verse
From the Tablets of God's decree[247]
In Your school.

O favor of universes, offer a pearl
From the sea of Divine understanding
To the one who made this land a home,
Peace and comfort to the fish in the sea.

The wave of that sea sometimes gives pearls;
Other times, carries ships.
With its favor,
There is a trace of joy and manner
In every creature, from Him.

Most parts of this sea
Are an act of prostration,
Like the one who gives thanks to God.
Time by time,
Its waves rise to do some service.

The seven oceans of this world
In front of this secret sea
Are like a person who bestows a kindness
Or a worshiping priest.

The sea which is full of pearls and coral
Is our long life, our Soul.
Our life becomes eternal.
There won't be any end for us,
Thanks to Your kindness.

O particle, if you once understand,
You'll become a companion to the torrent
Which carries you to the sea.
You won't get hurt on the way.

If you try to go your own way
And that torrent of Love,
Which covers everything,
Grabs your ear to pull you on the way,
You'll be saved and protected.

Müstef'ilün, Müstef'ilün,[248]
Now I should hide my sugar,
Because they send a bunch of parrots
To loot it.

Watch all these new kinds of sugar.
Hear the sounds which come from chewing.
These sugars do not have form,
Nor do the parrots have jaws or feet.
None of them is visible.

There is another sugar from God
That isn't in the sugar cane.
The parrot doesn't have the power to eat it,
Nor are men able to swallow it
Down their throats.

That sugar resembles Shems of Tebriz.
Neither can He be contained by the sky.
His sun rises in the land of wonder. [249]

133.

Verse 1712

O One who put a tent of hair
On the garden of earth!
O One who put fire in the material
And made a whole,
Adorned and ornamented Soul!

The roots of the trees
Were tied to the ground
Before You untied them.
You laid down pearl on the ground
Where roses were standing.

The bird who tells riddles
Learned to talk from You.
You give hundreds of wings
To the sick, pale falcon of Heart.

O One who gives life without death,
Provisions without food!
You give the best shield
For the arrow of death.

The Lover is like a pen
Which walks wobbling on this road.
In order to walk straight,
You draw a straight line.

It isn't surprising
That You made man from an animal, an oxen.
You made ambergris
Out of the water buffalo's left-over excrement.

The person who conquered the universe for You
Received hundreds of swords,
Hundreds of soldiers from their own particles,
Like sun and sunshine.

Angels prostrate themselves
In front of Adam.
Even the sky becomes a water carrier,
A slave for humans.

You gave power to the stars
And affect to the soil and stones.
You spread this power to the earth,
Then You built stairs,
Made a passage from Heart to sky.

You gave the temptation of lust to black dirt.
In order to give birth
And make delivery,
One bit of soil
Became the father; the other, mother.

You have the power to open doors
To the heavens from the grave.
You created the five senses in the body's grave
And opened the doors to the universe.

You hid hundreds of raindrops of compassion
In the anger of the father,
Hid hundreds of sparks of fire
In the Hearts of a generation of men.

You built a tent for the Soul
From the mantle
Made by our saliva, blood, bile and Love,
O my Sultan.

There will be a time
When this world will argue
With the One who listens and says,
"I've spoken words like the 'Fountain of Life.'
You have not heard because of your deafness."

O Shems of Tebriz,
Explain the meaning, hair by hair.
Since You made a head,
Give him hands and feet, too.

134.

O Sun of rebellion!
O Beauty who bows to no one!
You're in agreement
With the Milky Way up in the sky.
You've become friendly with people,
Like milk and honey.

O You've given joy to every particle,
Like the wine which adds Soul to Soul.
O You've merged and saturated the earth
With a rain of favors.

You've plunged in fire so much
That You've flamed, burned the fire.
We've looked for Your trace so much
That You've unified with the One
Whose trace cannot be found.

O secret of God,
Who has no wants,
O One who has no need for good or bad,
You've given up Your self.
You've merged with Absolute might.

You were searched for everywhere by Souls,
But no one ever got a smell of You.
They all became desperate;
Their Hearts were ruined.
Then suddenly, You joined them.

It's no wonder
That the same kind will unite.
Otherwise, different people cannot become one.
But You are not this or that.
Even so, You came to an understanding
With this, with that.

Both worlds are Your guests,
They sit around Your table.
You offer them hundreds of blessings.
You join the guests.

You've merged with Him so much
That He cannot differentiate himself from You.
How could He differentiate,
Since You merged like a body
United with the Soul?

You've become the beauty and freshness
Of this rose garden.
O great old man, be rejuvenated.
O arrow, you'll reach the target
Because you're joined to the bow.

O everyone's kingdom and destiny,
You've stolen everyone's belongings.
You came very quickly,
Staged a hold-up on our way,
But agreeing with the caravan,
Joined them, then left.

You thought that fate
Is to keep walking.
You agreed with the universe.
Soul is flying high.
So is the universe.

I admire Your kindness.
When stress becomes overpowering,
Like the butcher,
Who bends the lamb's head toward its hind legs,
You hold the head of stress
And bend it in the same way.

You taught Joseph-faced beauties
How to kill the Beloved.
You are the One who merged.
The devil is looking for thorns
Within the rose garden

The One who knows and understands,
Leave this alone.
Look at Him. Watch Him with the cleanest eyes.
You're freed from the particles of earth.
You've reached and merged with the sky.

O bird of Soul, you're free from the trap.
You've landed on the branch of the rose tree.
You're saved from the anxieties of the Heart,
Entered the heavens, reached that universe.

O Fountain of Life, honor of the water of vitality,
You came from the roof of the sky,
Ran around our roof, then merged
And flew through the gutter pipe.

How could a robber find You at night?
You're not at home.
You hid Your cane on the roof.
You made a deal with the watchman.

Tell the secret of this without words,
Without the alphabet of one hair to the other,
O One who, while talking, merges
And becomes one with the sounds and alphabet.

135.

O One who gives ecstasy
Better than eternal drunkeness
To the Soul, without a wine cup!
Come, if only for one moment.
Give us our blessing, that moment
Which is so clean of everything,
Including cleaness.
How long must we wait for that unique moment?

You are such a Sultan of plunder
That even the enemy is waiting to be pillaged,
Because of the greatness of Your pillage.

Is it His form or the form of the universe?
Why doesn't the Soul know this?
For sure, feet know
If the shoes fit him, belong to him.

Feet are comfortable in their own shoes.
Someone else's shoes will feel
Tight and uncomfortable.

The mind has this capability,
But is unable to withstand that moment
When it is jailed in this world.

The Soul also knows his peers, his friends,
Because in the world of Absence,
That knowledge is given to the Soul
According to his limits, his capacity.

This is just the same
As the grown-up clothes of the prince
Being hidden in the basement chest.

Open the lock of the Heart,
Walk toward the treasure.
If you have this treasure,
You'll have the answers
To all the questions in two worlds.

The tavern of man is the Heart
If you know what kind of drunkenness
You can have there.
But you are a little child yet.
Your feet are stuck in the mud.
You'll have to wait awhile.

Wait awhile, then luck
May bring a bunch of grapes.
Look. There is dust far away,
Raised like a flag.

On this flag is written,
"This is the proof, the evidence
Of the sign of Shems of Tebriz,
To whom all Tebriz and China
Are singing praises."[250]

136.

O unique Hasbek[251] rider,
You rode from the land of Soul
To the tavern,
Incited one against the other,
And went all the way to the square.

The Ones who stay in the sky
Pulled our ear.
You curl Your mustache
And ride Your horse toward them.

O One who, when He takes one step,
Goes beyond the two worlds,
Do You know to what place
You ride Your horse?

All modesty and rhymes
Have been ruined by Your love.
Since You've gone toward them,
No curtain is left.

When You ride toward the Soul, start looting,
The mind loses its mind.
Love becomes Your admirer.
Only one name lives in the body.

137.

Please, be content with the Beloved
One moment.
Give honor to the sky,
O One whose face
Is more beautiful than the moon!

His name, when mentioned between words,
Gives the drunkenness of aged wine.
Teach the translater how to please the Heart
For even one short moment.

The sea is a touch of humidity in Your palm.
Even with all Your genorsity,
You still deprive one confidant.
Don't. Put the watchman to sleep one moment.

Your Love is giving me a wine
Which cannot be described
And keeps putting opium in it.
How could the drunk
Who's been drinking this wine
Be able to show a trace from the One
Whose trace cannot be found?
How can he show a sign from Him?

Enlighten the world with Your face.
Make the eyes of fate drunk.
For one moment, take the troubles
Out of the universe's Soul.

O One who is a hundred times
Sweeter than the Soul,
How difficult to describe You with language!
Only the sufi can do that.
Bring that sufi for one moment.

I repent.
O mind, how would the sufi find the way to Him?
Hold your tongue.
Not every bird can fly on that side.

O sun of God, even the moon
Tears its colored shirt with Your Love.
O red colors of sunset,
Leave him alone for one moment,
For the Love of ruby-colored lips.

You should have only His Love in your Heart.
Don't take useless measures.
Don't stay any place for the night.
Annihilate all of your beings.

O the One whose rest and decisions are hidden
Around His search,
Safety and comfort in His fear!
The Soul desires You so much
That just to reach You
He left safety; he left mercy.

My body is like a bow;
My Heart is the bow string.
O Soul, aim high in the sky.
For a moment, put the ladder to the sky.

A young one in every place
Has grown old for no reason
Because of Your grief.
Show Your brow, so I can see the kingdom.
I'll reach eternity in one moment.
I won't grow old forever.

Look at this crying one.
Be true to Your own work for a moment,
My Sultan.
Be generous, be just, have pity.
Turn the head of Your horse this way.
Gallop here.

Come here for one moment.
Have the Soul chew sugar.
Show Your halo to our eyes for one moment.
We'll see You.

When I want to be jumped and thrown down,
I turn into an arrow
And fly over the village to get better.
Show me Your brow.
I will stretch that bow.

O raven of separation
Which has no essence, born from illusion,
When will you leave me and fly away
Like a raven?

O light which every eye with sight desires,
O light of the kingdom,
When will You ask, "I want such and such?"

O lion self, how can you be separated from Love?
O lion-natured self,
Throw this tasty food, this table
In front of the dogs. Throw it.

O One who has no idea about the Soul's wine,
How long will you be talking about skill, ability?
Even for one moment, throw that trap of bread
To the bottom of hell.

Where is the Sultan of time, Shemseddin,
The One to whom everyone
Is a slave and servant?
O Tebriz, for the Sultan
Whose kingdom is so obvious,
Build a temple, be His slave.

138.

O our King, our Sultan,
You came from the kingdom of the Sultan
Who has no beginning,
No end to His sovereignty,
Penetrated the Heart of the Moon
And conquered the flags of the King.

You rose from the land of Absence,
Which is the source of the working place
Of the Soul.
You came, causing hundreds of suns in the skies
To collide with each other.

You lit such a torch
That You burned night as well as day,
Made up such an excuse
That even goodness
Became shameful from malice.

O Venus of hundreds of Jupiters,
O Secret of God's favor,
O Fairy, in order to avoid jealousy,
Come to the land of Soul secretly.
Take the Soul's Heart in Your hand.

Oh Beauty of Beauties, You came
By swaying from side to side,
Because You are at the harem.
You are the desired beauty of the one who prays
And also the direction to the house of prayer.

His face, which shines with the
The Glory of the Creator,
Has matchless beauty.
The curly hair coming down to the forehead
Is adorned with Ahmets' taylasan.[252]
Nothing resembles the way His hair looks
And smells like black musk.

When Shems of Tebriz goes,
Soul follows Him like a shadow.
The earth He steps on
Is either salve for the eye
Or make-up for the light of eternity.

139.

O Heart, you're not telling
What has happened to you.
You've fallen in love,
Which adds life to your life.
Sometimes you become mad with grief;
Other times turn into blood with trouble.

When I talk about your love,
Lots of trouble appears
In the land of Absence.
O lucky, good-fortuned one,
Play until dawn.

When the time came to drink wine,
We became indebted up to our necks
Because of that wine.
No, no, leave this 'wine' word alone.
Watch the One who gets drunk
Without a glass and wine.

You insist like burning fire,
I'm spread like soil on the ground.
You sent fire to me. I'm burning.
O Beautiful, you are surely beautiful.

O Absence, attack existence.
Destroy, be drunk.
Give your heart to drunkenness.
Clap your hands, clap your hands.

"Oh moon," I said, "Look at us!
Watch the eyes which have turned into sea.
Don't go there. Look here!"
"Congratulations, how nice," he said.
"Look at Love."

342

O nightingale, talk about the rose garden.
Say something about that cypress,
Tell about this pregnant branch.
Don't hide. Tell it like it is.

Don't look at forms all the time.
See the graceful Soul
That earth turned into sky,
With the sparkle of the Archangel Gabriel.

Forms are like shields
In the hand of the painter.
They hide His eyes and face.
Shapes are like drapes.
The One who makes the shapes
Is behind the curtain of Azer.[253]

140.

O my Beautiful,
You are the moon, You are Jupiter.
The moon turns around Your face
And worships You.
The sun, the sky are whirling with Your Love.

O my God, am I looking for You,
Or are You looking for me?
What a shame for me
That 'I' stays with 'am.'
As long as I cannot free myself from me,
I am one, You are another.

O the One who surrounds me, surrounds us,
Sheds the blood of us and me and both,
Makes someone appear in the middle!
But He is neither a man nor a fairy.

It's alright if the foot doesn't exist.
The foot takes us to thorns anyway.
It's alright if the head doesn't exist.
The head makes duality and disbelievers anyway.

There is water running in the creek.
Other water is frozen on the side.
This goes fast, the other very slow.
Put your mind into your head.
Run fast, so that you won't be frozen.

The sun tells the stone,
"In order to make you a jewel,
I shine on you and enlighten you,
So that you'll be free from being a stone."

The unfading sun of Love
Also reflects on your Heart
To raise you from manhood.

The sultan says to the falcon,
"I cover your eyes
So you'll feel cold to your peers
And see only my face."

The sun tells the unripe grape
"I came to your kitchen
So you won't sell the vineyard.
You'll learn how to make Halva." [254]

The falcon says, "Yes," to the sultan, says,
"I obey your order. I see only your face,
Dream only of you. I'll become
The slave by Heart."

The rose tells the garden,
"I put everything I have in front of you
So that you'll give up everything that's yours.
Stay, eat and drink with us."

If anyone takes gold from here,
Goes and spends it with another beauty,
He has to be a donkey.
He sits awry, but talks straight.

Jesus turns your copper into gold,
Then gold into jewelry, even makes your jewelry
Better than the moon or sun.

He's not like a penniless customer.
He makes you aware of the secret,
"God has bought."[255]
If you are Joseph, you'll get the smell
From that shirt.

Fresh dates are given to us from the dry branch,
Just like Mary.
Holiness is destined in the cradle without asking,
Just like Jesus.

Look at the grape which has no garden.
Watch the glory shine without night.
See God's blessed kingdom
Devoid of all troubles and fights.

My fiery face warmed the earth's bath.
Don't cry like children.
Look at the pictures
On the glass of the bath.[256]

You'll see tomorrow
That his face became food for snakes and rats,
That his narcissus eyes became a window
For the ants to come and go through.

The wall stays in the dark
And doesn't read the verse,
"Really, we will return to Him,"[257]
As long as the moonlight doesn't warm it
And the moon doesn't reflect on it.
If you see, have sight, look at it that way.

Either go to Tebriz and get pleasure from Shems
Or believe the One telling all this.

141.

Verse 1818
Terci-Bend

O Soul, the One who is pulling us
From earth to the green sky,
How beautifully You are pulling us!
Pull us faster!

I woke up so beautifully today,
Making all kinds of noise, struggling.
Today, I'm even more exalted,
Because You're pulling me better today.

You're throwing all the thirsty ones
Into the river today,
Pulling Abraham to water and fire with Zün-nûn.[258]

People have been burned and ruined today.
Their eyes have been kept on You.
Who is the one You'll be pulling first?
They're all waiting to see him.
Will You be taking him on Your arm?

O the Source of the Beauty of Beauties,
You are something else today.
How nicely You took
The Heart from the chest,
The mind from the head.

O sky, you are a tent.
O earth, you are a nice country.
O sun, you are spreading pearls.
O night, you are making ambergris.

O early dawn, how beautifully becoming
Your light is.
O breeze, what a nice friend you are.
O sun killing the stars!
O moon pulling the armies!

O rose, you're going to the rose garden.
O bud, growing secretly,
O cypress, how beautifully
You suck the nectar from under the ground.

O Soul, You are peace to the body,
Wine to the flesh.
O religion, you are my keys.
O Love, You are lively, crossing people's path.
O mind turning the book pages!

O wine, you are the one who gets rid of grief,
Salve for our wounds.
O beautiful Cupbearer, You are the One
Who drinks oceans with the cup.

O morning breeze, you are the messenger
Who brings news from the Beloved
Every morning.
You take such gifts from His ambergris hair.

O earth, you are under every step.
In your Heart you hide so many rose gardens.
The water runs, making its head like feet.
You run, but you gather pearls from the sea.

O fire, which wears a ruby kaftan,
You blaze from Love.
You open your mouth like a dragon
And swallow everything.

Tercî means that You pull us to the heights,
Grab the Soul, pulling us to the place
Where Souls have been grown, matured.

* * * * * * * *

You are pulling the Jesus of Soul
To the star of the Pleiades.
There is no up, no down in such a universe.
You are leading Soul high,
Highest to the most exalted God.

Like Moses, You brought springs out of the eye,
Pulling the Moses of Soul to Mount Sinai.

Keep pulling this undecided mind.
In what a nice way You carry
This blood-thirsty Soul.

You are the Soul of our Soul.
You are the essence of all.
From there, You are pulling our self to Us.

We came like *lâ*,[259] upside down.
You keep pulling us from nothing
To the land of *illâ*.[260]

Self is nothing but a house of idols,
But with You, it becomes a Mescid-i Aksâ.[261]
You're pulling mind,
Which is nothing but a small candle,
To the roof of the sky.

Sultans have put all the guilty ones in jail.
You pull them out of jail
And take them to joy and pleasure.

You fill the body that You've purified
With musk and ambergis,
Give the wings of a phoenix to a fly.

You make the body,
Which resembles a dirty raven,
Like a carcass,
And, at the same time, having Soul
Which resembles a clean parrot chewing sugar,
Pull him high in the sky.

You give fresh dates
From the dry branch of the date palm
To the tired, sorrowed Mary.

You pull Joseph, who is soiled with blood,
From the bottom of the well.
Every moment, you're pulling him
Through secret roads to the heights of the sky.

When Jonah was caged inside the fish,
You took him to Your side,
Like a pearl from the bottom of the sea.

You set the table of angels
At the assembly of Heart's drunks
And offer Jesus' meals
To the drunk of Hearts.

This is another Tercî.
You are bringing the heaven of Soul
In front of the guest with Your kindness, favors.

*****

You pull the troubled hearts of lovers
To the place of remedy
And lead every longing, thirsty one
Toward the Fountain of Life.

350

How could You pull the one
Who doesn't have an understanding Heart
And who isn't a Sultan?
You pull every human like that.

You are the Sultan of Sultans.
You are endless compassion.
You are the One who set a table of favor
In the time of scarcity.

You show such modesty
To the few poor, needy ones.
You are just a humble person
Taking meals to the Sultan.

You are filling their baskets
With rubies and pearls
And carrying those baskets
Like the rain carries straw.

There is the order, "God is calling." [226]
Come, free the ones in the dungeon.
But they fall in sorrow
As though You were calling them to the dungeon.

You scare the pharoah with snakes,
But in reality Your kindness and Your favor
Save him from himself, which resembles a snake.

With Your kindness, You said to the pharoah,
"I am taking you to the throne, the crown.
Don't resist, let Me pull you,
Because you cannot do it."

The pharoah said, "This bond is from You.
Moses is a pretext. Pull me like Moses, secretly."

He answered, "If he were Moses,
Why did the staff became a dragon?
His palm shone like the moon.
You turned your head from forgiveness.

"We sent Moses to Shuayb,[263] uninvited.
Why are you jealous and greedy
Like a helpless lover?

"Moses did not complain,
Served Shuayb for ten years as a shepherd.
How would you be, if called shepherd?"

O Shems of Tebriz,
Oratory has been refined by You.
Boiled, overflowing with bubbles,
This bubble jumped over the head,
Because You are pulling him to Saturn.

That is another Tercî.
Soul, You pull every moment.
If You do so slowly,
The trouble of my Heart increases.

****

O One who pulls and leads us,
You are the sun.
We resemble humidity;
You pull us to the heights.

You give life once more
To these dead bones.
You are taking on a cruise
The ones who are jailed in sorrow and grief.

Soul was drinking wine before
With angels in the sky.
Soul is clapping His hands,
Because You're pulling him back up there again.

O Sun, O Moon, O Brightness!
You are the place for safety and comfort.
Stage a hold-up on our road.
How nicely you do it. Pull us nicely.

O Sun who protects the good one,
O young fate, fresh destiny,
You hold us like a water bag,
Taking us to that river.

When I saw Your jar,
I pawned my turban, my Heart.
I told thought, "Go away,"
Because You are pulling me to Love.

O mind, you make me exist.
O Love, You make me drunk.
Although You humiliate me,
You are taking me
To the Greatest of the Great Almighty.

O Love, give Your order.
Separate us from everyone except You.
O torrent, you are taking us
To the sea with the cascade.

O Soul, come and confess.
O flesh, go and deny.
O Absence, hang me on the gallows,
Because You are taking me to essence.

Everyone pulls everything to themselves,
Good or bad,
Yet You pull us toward ourselves.

O head, you become head with His Grace.
O feet, you become feet
With His kindness acting as a guide.
But You turned away from Him.
Why do you raise your head with arrogance
And pull your feet with laziness?

O head, if you want the sky,
Put your head on the ground.
O feet, if you want to go to the valley,
Don't get stuck in the mud.

O eye, don't look at the people.
O ear, don't hear good or bad.
O mind, don't be a donkey-brain.
You are going to Jesus.

I swear to God, you are really pulling nicely,
Without hand and dagger.
You are pulling us to the temple
Of timelessness and spacelessness,
Leading us in the direction of no direction.

142.

Verse 1874

O friend, if you do good to others,
You better yourself a hundred times.
Even if you turn your face this way,
Maybe you will get to know Us.

I spread water on the ground
To settle the dust
And decorated every place.
Even if I forgive your sins,
Maybe you will get to know Us.

I have made you out of nothing,
Put you on the throne.
I gave you a mirror so you can work for us.
Maybe you will get to know Us.

O son of My pillar, My foundation!
O one who is asking help from Me,
Come now, see My favors
Maybe you will get to know Us.

Be wine to My cup.
Become a stranger to yourself, feel My pain.
If you stay in the same house with My suffering,
Maybe you will get to know Us.

O Sultan's son, be just.
Liberate yourself from your self.
Remember the day of death.
Maybe you will get to know Us.

The phoenix of Soul flys off
Just like an arrow from the bow.
You such and such, think about that.
Maybe you will get to know Us.

Fasten your ties with your religion.
Keep your oath.
Fall in Love with your faith.
Maybe you will get to know Us.

O the one who collects gold and silver,
Falls in love with every sweet pair of lips,
Come and see what real Beauty is.
Maybe you will get to know Us.

I've sown the seeds of faithfulness.
I've drawn wonderful pictures
And opened so many curtains.
Maybe you will get to know Us.

143.

Verse 1884

O One who rides the horse of eternity
And leaves this temporary monastery,
You know Your way.
You're going to the place You know.

Without becoming friends
With material things and symptoms,
Without falling into the trap,
Without slowing down with illness,
You're going from bitterness to sweetness
From deprivation to Your intention.

You are the Soul of Souls.
That's the way You're going;
Not like the mind which gathers bait;
Not like the self, full of hatred and grudges;
Not like the souls of the creatures
Which live on earth.

O One who makes the web of fate,
O One who shines like the moon,
The One who found a track, a trace on the road,
You're going to the One
Who has no track, no trace.

O One who is overwhelmed by His Love,
O One who has gone
Beyond himself with wine,
You are going from Medrese,[264]
Where His names have been taught,
To their meanings.

You should not give the impression to people
That You're going without gifts.
Your manners, which resemble
The water in the creek,
Give smell and color to time.

At night, hundreds of caravans go
To the sky from this world.
You're going alone.
But by Yourself, You are hundreds of caravans.

O Sun of that world,
Why are You hiding in one particle?
O Sultan of Sultans,
You're going like a guard.

You cast spells beyond day and night
So that eyes will think
You're going somewhere, to some country.

O Favor of the unknown,
How many times You've come dressed like spring!
O Absolute Justice,
How many times You've appeared,
Then disappeared in the fall season!

Get out of these forms.
Take this cover off Your face.
How long will You act
Like a shepherd in human form?

O One whose sign appears,
But whose essence is hidden like the Soul,
O One who became slave and servant
At the temple of earth,
When am I going to see You secretly,
Like the Soul?
You are going to the world of silence.

144.

O Joseph, whose name is beautiful,
O beautiful charmer, you won't find
Any companion on the journey.
Don't be separated from the reason of Jacob
To keep from falling into the well.

The dog is the one who sleeps idle
In front of every door.
The donkey is the one who gets tired
And goes to any tent it sees.

Where is this Love, this greed
Which comes from the Heart?
Only the One who makes the Heart knows;
The One who understands
Makes you understand.

Lean over, don't leave the egg.
Watch like a bird.
But once your Heart's egg is hatched
And the chick comes out,
Drunkenness, union, and laughter
Are all for you.

Uncle, no one but Him
Has the shirt for this and that favor;
The rest are all poor.
Hang on.
Entreat the Sultan of Sultans
With both hands.

Fall into His grief, follow sorrow.
Walk with fire until evening,
Like the sun.
At night, keep turning nicely around His roof,
Like the moon.

Those stars keep guard around His roof
With their batons until morning.
I swear to God, it's a great temple,
It's a great door.

Those prophets who turn their faces to the sky
Are saved from the traps of earth
And from the stupid people
Who attribute a partner to God.

They are trapped in the other world
The way iron is attracted to a magnet,
An armless, legless piece of straw
Which flies toward amber.

Know for sure that without His favor
No food ever grows.
Without His order, His creation,
Not even a shadow would fall to earth.

Souls are like drunk camels
Which wander around the desert
When they hear the sound 'travel.'[265]
He is the desert Arab. He says, "Uh, uh,"
And makes the camels kneel anywhere He wants.

If the Remil [266]maker of the Soul
Casts the sand of Truth
On the Heart's signboard,
All the numbered sands turn into real gold.

Friends, go nicely on your journey.
A kind of doctor came to this earth,
Who brings every death to life
And opens the eyes of all born blind.

All these things could happen,
But when He lifts the veil from His face,
It won't be Venus
Or the sounds of the professional cryers.

Be silent! If you are a nightingale,
Fly to the rose garden.
Even the nightingale lands on thorns,
But that is very seldom.

145.

Sounds are coming from the sky every moment,
But no one hears them
Except the Ones who are in a state of ecstasy.

O the one who bends his head down
Like a donkey,
Drink less of this water,
Eat less of this grass.
For a moment, lift your head up.
Maybe you can see a sign or proof.

Nowadays, the Cupbearer opens
The top of the jar of sky.
He has an army of Souls
And flags from the wine.

Where is that lion-hearted one in this world,
That brave hero?
Who will meet him?
He will be brave enough to hunt lions.
The one who drinks wine with the brave Sultan
Has to be Sultan.

What a pity it is that the ear
Which attributes a partner to God
Is open, but doesn't hear the voice
Coming from the sky!
The soul that hasn't received
Peace and Love from God,
What a helpless and lost soul that is!

Would it be possible
That just one night,
You wouldn't have the Soul say,
"O my God,"
That you would pull and free him
From the dungeon of the body,
And be led to a large space?

When you untie the rope from your feet,
You'll fly to the sky.
Like the sky, you'll be immune
From wear and tear and all hazards.

You'll be saved from the sword of death.
You'll join the Union of Soul.
You'll be in such a garden
That fall's looting will never take place.

I'll be silent.
The silence that Love would tell to Love,
That would be a narration
Which would feed the Soul
And have no end.

146.

$\mathcal{A}$ Heart-catching smell has come from the sky,
Saving every tired, broken-hearted prey
From the trap of the flesh.

Every bird has gained hundreds of wings,
Keeps flying to the star of Pleiades.
Every weight, every mountain
Has started flying with its own weight.

Look at the birds of Abraham.[267]
Even though they were torn to pieces,
They came back flying.

I asked, "Oh particle, you have no wings, no head.
How do you fly?"
He said, "With the wind of Love."

From now on, you can hear no yell
But the shrill pipe from the city.
You can hear no cry
But the harp from the house.

The tambur[268] says,
"Life is our life,"
Then starts all the melodies.
The bee of the soul
Learned architecture from that honey.

Today, the Cupbearer,
Whose offers are as generous
And endless as the sea,
Has given up greatness
And mixed with ordinary people.

He whispers instigations
To the ear of chance and fate.
But today, we are saved from this sorrow,
O my God!

The singer of the Soul sings and blows
Like the Son of Mary.
The Cupbearer attacks like God's lion
Again and again,
Then offers wine,
Then attacks repeatedly.

If He breaks a few idols,
He then carves hundreds more immediately.
If He breaks two or three jars,
It doesn't matter.
His ability, His art in making
New jars from kneaded mud
Hasn't been decreased.

O nightingale, you learned
All these beautiful melodies
Because of the rose.
But once you reach the Beloved,
You'll be with Him.
You will say very little
And forget all of them.

147.

Verse 1931

If you go to the garden of Heart,
You'll have beautiful perfume like a rose.
If you fly to the sky,
Your face will turn into a moon like the angels.

You'll turn into light
Even if He burns you like oil.
You'll become like hair because of grief,
But they'll put you at the head of the table.
Like a candle, you'll illuminate the assemblies.

You'll become a Sultan.
You'll become supreme sovereignty,
Heaven, and an angel at the door of heaven.
You'll become sky and faith.
You'll turn into a lion
And, at the same time, a gazelle.

You'll leave place.
You'll go the the land of Absence.
You'll separate from yourself.
You'll go alone, walking without riding,
Without feet, like water in the river.

You'll become One like Heart and Soul,
You'll keep appearing even if you are invisible.
You'll become bitter-sweet, like wine.

You'll be free from the qualities
Of wetness and dryness, like Jesus.
You'll pierce the turbulence
And make a road of it.
You'll be free of dimensions;
Every side will become one for you.

You'll be free from desires
And the fancy of your insides.
You'll become empty.
You'll stay alive without breath.
You'll be plunged into the sea of Ya Hu, [269]
And then you'll quit saying, "Ya Hu."

You'll turn sweet into bitter
And hear all, from a distance.
When you reach the ninth level of the sky,
You won't be a curtain to the light.

Be a Sultan with a kingdom.
Reach the height. Become a moon.
How long will you keep searching
By saying, "Coo-coo," like the dove?

You'll become a window for every house.
You'll be a rose garden in every field.
If you leave your self, drop your existence,
You'll become Me without me.

Don't take the lead. Don't brag.
Be joyful, bend your head,
Like a branch of the peach tree.
Smile. Be beautiful.

You won't ask for light.
You won't need your self.
You'll look after
The feeding and care of the poor,
Like the Sultan.
You'll look for darkness, like the moon.

You won't look for Soul;
You'll give Soul.
You'll find a remedy for every ill.
Don't look for salve for your wounds.
You'll be salve for all wounds.

148.

I want peace from You,
Understanding and Union.
You showed me a sign,
Said something about peace yesterday.

The Soul became so happy, so cheerful
That it started singing and playing.
That's His most important job,
To sing songs about peace.
Is there anything more important than that?

When the Soul is angry with someone,
The world becomes a jail for him.
When does the idea of getting along with body
Come to Soul, O my God?

When you're angry with someone,
You head somewhere else.
But if your head is angry with you,
What happens to peace?

If my Heart should kiss the hand of Union
While searching for You,
At that time it will also kiss the dust
Of the feet of peace
And keep kissing.

The goodness which the body does
Is always from the kindness of Soul.
Whenever I was generous,
This was the generosity of peace.

I cried like winter rain.
No leaves, no fruits. I am naked, new.
I want to dress in the kaftan of peace
And roar suddenly.

I would be Sultan.
To become Sultan to the Sultans,
I will do favors, even for the moon.
I will smile when I see the face of peace.

O Soul of hundreds of gardens
And hundreds of greens,
Come, give Your honor to this country.
When there is no room for peace
Because of my bad thoughts, bad measures,
Even then, be kind to me.

Come, give this charm to the earth
From unthinkable, unbelievable spring.
That way, there won't be a fog of grief
In the sky of peace.

It isn't good to have these fights and struggles
Against the sea of Soul.
It isn't good to do evil things,
To try and boast
Against the greatness of peace.

O one who does things beyond modesty,
Be silent. Don't even say one thing
With the tip of your lips
So that the prayer for peace becomes modest.

149.

His image in the heart offers endless favors
So that you won't look anywhere else.

If you step out of this six-doored chapel, [270]
You'll meet the sufi whose fate is clean;
You'll reach His ecstasy.

You have a secret door.
Every night you fly away through that door.
Don't look for six directions, six doors.

They tie an imaginary string to your feet
When you fly
So that you won't get lost.
They pull you back every morning
With that string.

This world looks like a womb.
That's why you're fed by blood.
Return to the dungeon of this womb
Until your creation is complete.

When the Soul grows wings,
The shell of the body is broken.
In order to show Cafer,
Become Ca'fer-i Tayyâr. [271]

150.

Spring has come, see?
The gardens and meadows are full
Of Houris[272] and fairies.
It's just like Solomon
Showing his ring to the army.

Rum-faced charmers were born
In the land of Ethiopia.
Just like you, many beautiful Moslems
Become faithful, cease to be infidels.

Look at the rose garden.
Watch the flowers of the pomegranate.
See the reflection of the Beloved on the water.
Admire these drunk, narcissus eyes.
Admire these red, rosebud lips.

Look at the petals of the rose.
How nicely gold and silver mix with each other.
They're like matchless jewels
Which came from no jeweler's art.

See the rose in the Soul of the nightingale.
See universal intelligence in that rose.
Fly from color to colorlessness.
Maybe you can find the road there.

The rose loots the mind.
Other flowers make signs as though saying,
"The One who made this painting, this form
Is here, right behind this curtain."

O One who gives peace to war,
Who brings water out of stone,
How do You bring all these colors
Out of this ordinary soil?

There is freshness in the branches,
Greatness and height in the cypresses,
Hundreds of beauties in the rose.
But, O Soul, you are altogether different.

It isn't the place for garden, valley and rose,
Nor the time for food and wine glasses,
Not even for Soul and universal intelligence,
Because you are better and more beautiful
Than the Soul of Soul.

151.

If the garden knew Him,
Blood would drip from its fresh branches.
If the mind understood Him,
A river would overflow from its eyes.

If that beautiful piece of Moon
Ever rose and appeared
From the circle of sun,
Every particle would become
Leylâ and Mecnun.[273]

If His treasures of mind
Would ever reflect down from one corner.
Hundreds of treasures of Karun[274]
Would be in every ruin.

If the Beauty reflected in the Heart
Were seen in the eyes,
Every person who washes the dirt from his face
Would become Seyh Zün-nûn.[275]

O merchant who looks around,
How long will you keep looking?
If to reach the Beloved were so cheap,
The Beloved would come forward with that look.

When a new guest comes,
That blessing in the world is enough.
If more people come to earth,
More blessings will come.

152.

Verse 1977

*L*ast night I saw the secret of Heart
On the face of the stone-hearted,
Ruby-lipped Charmer
Who offers belief to blasphemy,
Increases the faith of unbelievers.

Who will talk about Soul and Heart
In front of such a Beloved?
Who will mention gold and silver
In the presence of that silver statue of Beauty?

If Love had a mouth,
The whole world would become a morsel.
If Love had a door,
The Soul of Sultans
Would become doorkeeper at that door.

I used to hear people say, "Heart, Heart!"
It's happened to me so that I understand.
O the Beautiful to His Beauty,
Soul and Heart become ashamed.
O the Charmer with His love,
Even Düldül [276]
Becomes a donkey stuck in the mud.

O Soul, come gather pearls.
O Soul, come and see the Beauty,
Mercy from this disaster, from grief,
O Moslems.

Where is the body
That would spread under His cavalry of sorrows?
Where is the head that wouldn't bend
At the assembly of such a Sultan?

Earth will become green and beautiful.
Spring has come, friends,
Like the time of Union with my Beloved.
It is so sweet, so charming, like His ruby lips.

Every moment His face is asking me
If I have any beautiful-faced Beloved like Him.
My heart is asking Him,
"Do You have any servant like me?"

Friends, let's go to the rose garden.
Spring is here.
But You are my spring,
I don't look at anything else.

Flowers and fruits have air,
Tone and gracefulness.
But we are like water lillies around Your face
Which looks like a rose garden.

Nightingales are playing tambourines.
Leaves of the trees keep clapping their hands.
Every bud is asking,
"Is there a fresher, more beautiful bud, than I?"

That kind, gracious, green spring
Has come dragging its skirt,
Swaying from side to side
So that the garden would be adorned.
Birds have taken wing and are flying.

Spring has come so that people will be happy.
Out of obstinacy to the blind
Who don't see this face,
To the deaf
Who don't hear this voice,
Spring has come.
Our Beloved becomes Soul to our Soul.

If He is the Sultan in one place,
The rest of the Sultans
Become slaves and servants.
If He is the Beloved in one place,
Every Heart turns into Lover's grass. [277]

The specter of my Beloved
Walks, swaying in the Heart,
A moon which has
The greatest exaltation and beauty,
With favor and kindness
Like a magnificent Sultan.

153.

I was looking for a buyer for my words,
Wanted someone who would have them.
Now, I want You to take my words.

I've carved so many idols
To deceive everyone,
But I'm tired of being Âzer.[278]
Today, I am the drunk of Abraham.

Such an idol has come my way
That has no color, no smell.
I lost my words just by looking at Him.
You find another master for the house of idols!

I've given up the store, left words.
I appreciate the value of insanity.
I've given up the mind.

When a form comes to my Heart, I say,
"Go away, O One who made me lose my way."
If it moves slowly,
I crack and break it into pieces.

The One who becomes His Mecnun, [279]
Cannot deserve Leylâ.
The One who comes from there,
Whose Soul belongs there,
His place is under the flag.

378

154.

If turning those two to Kible [280] would go away
From mind and Soul for one moment,
Our mind would be Adam,
Our self would be Eve.

If Adam hadn't descended
From the canopy of Heart
And gotten stuck in this mud,
His holy teaching would be better
Than the attributes of God.

The one who falls in doubt and says,
"I don't believe that,"
If he would have believed
And surrendered like Abraham,
His shadow,
Which falls on the ground upside down,
Would have become a sun in the sky.

If the existence of body were annihilated,
Self would become exalted.
His head would reach the sky.
When completely he became Nothing,
He would reach the Union of Existence.

If there weren't weakness in the eyes
Of the self who looks like a bat,
Instead of one sun,
A hundred suns would rise
And add Soul to Souls.

If good and bad were the same
At the final time in God's place,
The devil would be as beautiful
As moon-faced Gabriel.

If man knew the secret,
Evil and benevolence wouldn't appear.
Everything he didn't know
Would appear, become obvious.

This sense of ours
Which looks and watches everything
Is in our trap, becomes our prisoner.
Since he doesn't see the truth of anything,
I wish he would go blind.

The feeling of the banal self
Is like a fly which has landed
On the side of the basin.
If the fly would choose a better place for landing,
It would immediately turn into a phoenix.

The stars resemble the bowls, those golden bowls.
They are adorned for the greedy ones.
It would be better
If they were not adorned or decorated.

Be silent. The word comes
From the land of Absence.
If your eyes are over there,
How can you fly there with words?

Because of Shems of Tebriz,
Know for sure that every particle
Is the light of certainty.
If the pleasure were in the talking and saying,
Every particle would start talking.

155.

Verse 2010

O brightness of every Heart's garden!
O window of every house!
Your sun shines in every particle,
Like a piece of pearl.

O One who comes to aide
Every helpless one,
The place for every homeless one,
You correct everything untidy.
You are the purpose and moral
Of every story.

O longing of the tall, straight cypress!
O brightness of the Sultan of Sultans!
I plead of You, give to Lovers
A Lover deserved by Lovers.

Your Love is in every head.
Your wine is on every lip.
Without the abundance of Your sherbet,
The world would become an empty glass.

Every king is Your pawn,
A lousy prey of Your falcon.
O the One who changes
Everyone and everything,
One situation to the other,
Becomes the chain for every insane one.

There is a fire for every light,
A thorn for every rose.
There is a snake in the ruins
To protect every treasure.

O One whose rose garden
Doesn't have thorns!
O One whose clean light has no fire!
There is no snake, no snake bite,
No teeth marks around Your treasure.

You set forth such drink,
Sow hundreds of seeds for testing.
You haven't left one rational man in our town.

Thoughts, arts, talents are all beautiful
Because they've taken color from Your Love.
Harp players play until dawn
In front of the rising moon of Your sky.

Wisdom and insanity are mixed with each other,
Joined and spread hundreds of appetizing meals
On Your way.
Thought is like a comb
Plunged into Your curly black hair.

O One whose eyes resemble narcissus,
Sleep becomes a thorn to my eye.
I see lots of dreams when I'm awake,
But I see behind the loaded bale.

Even if he has sour yogurt,
The groceryman's Heart
Is still with the customer.
His lips closed, he sits and waits
At the corner of the store,
Awake until morning.

In the morning, he runs for profit
And starts bargaining.
In the end, because of his customer,
His dried mints come to life
And become green, fresh mint.

O one who leaves the field
And sows wheat in the garbage place,
In the barren land!
O one who thinks light is a window!
You resemble a moth.

Some day He will dress you,
Give you power of description, explanation,
Join your particles with universal intelligence
And offer you a Beloved.

Be silent. You are saved from that.
You've jumped out of those traps.
You gave your Heart and Soul
To this seducing charmer.

156.

It's only dawn, and the Cupbearer
Has already filled the glass.
He is as beautiful and bright
As the stars of Ursa Minor,[281]
Great as the cypress,
And sugar-lipped as a piece of the Moon.

His eyes are drunk. His curly hair,
Coming down on his forehead,
Resembles a trap.
He is help for the helpless.
The glass in His hand
Is a remedy for the sick one.

Black-eyed Houris[282] dance
In front of the sprinkling fountain,
Holding their harps on their arms
And playing at left and right
In the garden full of jasmine.

O sweet Cupbearer, pick up the glass
In spite of all the trouble and grief.
For the Soul of Alî[283] and Abu-l Alâ,[284] offer wine.

Turn like the sun in the sky, spread jewels.
Offer drink to the thirsty of this mean world,
To the occupants of this land of mud.

O the one who makes magic, who has talent,
O the one who is in the hand of insanity,
The time for work has arrived.
We are already the most competent ones
For that work.

I threw off the dress of modesty once.
I drank a glass, started Love-play
With a cruel, conceited, playful Beauty.

Even the ones in the sky
Are drunk from the smell of that wine.
Their heads are dizzy.
Every great person is prostrating
In front of my moon-faced Beauty
Like a drunk in ecstasy.

The seas of wine are flowing here and there.
Fifty rivers are in every garden.
Hit this jar on the stone and break it
For the obstinacy of mad people

Blessings and the elixir of Absence are raining.
The Sultans of drunkenness
Are met with large armies

If you see the ones who are passing
Above the roof,
You will tear down the tent of daily struggle,
Throw it in the fire.

The one who's called drunk
Goes like a ship up and down,
Wobbling on rough seas.
He goes like timber, awry, gnarled.

I ask, "O busy brave
Whose Soul has been saved from all ailment,
There is no door, no window.
How could you have freed yourself
From the dungeon of death?

"How have you been freed
From this bitter, sour earth;
From this old firmament who eats his own child;
From this place where he tells stories
And at the same time keeps silent,
A slave and at the same time a master?"

He told me, "The Sultan of the world
Secretly offered me a glass.
Once I drank, I turned into a star
Which goes around that town of Soul."

The entrance and exit are both concealed
In this world of trials.
They're hidden, well-covered
From men and women
At the wish of God.

Watch and see. There is no opening, no door.
How did I pass through?
How did I get out?
I'm like water
Which comes from a stone without a spring.

O taste of sugar,
Give some from this big earthern jar.
Like a mother, nurse me.
Pull, pick me up from the cradle.

O all the possessions,
The joy and pleasure of wise men!
O the One who adds more wonder
To the wonders of narcissus!
O the One who give sustenance
To that muddy world and those who live there,
The purpose of every idle one!

The thoughts of troubled ones
Are prostrating because of that wine
Which saves the person
From the guard, from thieves,
And the rest of the ordinary people.

O the glass which searches the Soul
And looks after the comfort of the wounded ones!
O the Cupbearer who has a face like the sun
And who keeps bleeding every star!

O One who gives sustenance to Hearts,
O One who becomes Soul
To the good and no-good ones!
You are the One who catches and loots
And, at the same time, overpraises and calms.
You are straight sometimes,
Then reverse and become one with whom
It's hard to get along.

You give life to these forms.
You are the sound of Gabriel's trumpet.
You turn this world into the Day of Judgement,
Incite everyone against each other.
Your chain is like a necklace,
Every cabbar [285] gives Him honor.

You took away the smartest thought
From the Soul,
Diverted, dismissed the mind.
You gave smartness to the silly fool,
Made him tricky and deceitful.

He attacks the master, the pasha
To cut the neck of doubt,
To beat time on the head of mind,
Or to make a tune on the order of the deceitful.

Enough! Be silent, join the crowd.
Come where men and women are together.
You also make shapes and figures
At the place of the solitude of the Master
Who makes statues out of mud.
Then you break and throw all those figurines.

You talk and, at the same time, are silent
Like a rose.
You don't make a face.
You are at the top corner
Of the house of the Heart.
At the same time, You are at the highest summit
Like a flying bird.

157.

All our belongings have been stolen
By a gentle, gracious, graceful charmer.
His deceits have not left
Even one carpet in the mosque.

The mantle of fate has been torn in ten pieces
Because of Him.
Kamer's[286] moon is pierced because of him.
What would happen if someone
As naive as I am
Were to fall into His hand?

He put fire to our aloe tree.
Our smoke went up to the sky.
The Cupbearer got rid of our useless works,
Wiped them out with that unseen wine.

It makes things difficult, staying at sea.
The Soul is telling the story of Heart.
Where is the Lover who gives his Heart?

The Lover who gives his Heart
Is not like you who goes about everywhere,
Then falls in one corner.
The true Lover has patience and persistence.

You are sad and sorrowful.
You've fallen into grief.
How can you be a Lover who has given his Heart?
You're either caught in the desire of a whore
Or caught in the anxiety of a pimp.

Shame on your beard, your cluttered beard.
In the end, you close your eyes
And open your mouth
To a lot of nonsense.

A good mind belongs on the other side,
Quick to see the outcome.
It is cleansed from greed, from lust.
It is ready to be a Lover.

Be silent. My Heart's bird
Is flying fast to the green.
It cannot be pawned to the book
Kept in a small room.

158.

$\mathcal{A}$ deceitful, pickpocket
Has grabbed my skirt,
Pulling me toward an idol house.
I'm following this blood-thirsty one,
Like a skirt.

He pulls me up one minute;
The next, he lets me down.
One moment he makes himself drunk;
That drunk thinks only of himself.

I am in his hand, like a small crystal ball.
Like a fish, I am in his net.
I bend down to the well of Babel
Because of his magician's eyes.

He is my divinity, my humanity,
He is my two angels.
For the ones who get involved in bad deeds,
He is my ruby, he is my coral.

You look like beautiful water.
A moon in the sign of fire.
But you are a marble Heart
In the chest of the Beloved, like a rock.

I will tell you the secret
Of that world's treasure,
But give me time, a little time
So that I can come to myself.

I took the jar to the river
With the image of Your face.
I saw the reflection of light
Like a star on the water.

I said to myself,
"What I was looking for in the sky,
I found on the earth."
God's favor suddenly becomes help
For the helpless one.

I'm thanking God at the garden of Union.
In my hand is a sword made in India.
I will settle with the light
Of the rose-faced One.

I used to be bent down like a bow,
Under grief and sorrow.
Those times are gone.
My body was like a bone
In the hand of every greedy person, then.

My old bow became new with the order to exist.
It came from the curl of the Sultan's monogram.
Jesus started talking,
Even when He was tied to the cradle.

Such a fire was dropped in the Heart
That no bad person could stand in front of me,
No renegade could rebel.
There is no self left
That could be the source of malice.[287]

The world of Lovers is beautified.
The time has come for Lovers to be united.
Their hearts have been freed
From all instigators and troublemakers.

Soul, tasteful, graceful Soul,
Is turning above the arch, like fate.
It cannot come down
And make the lower place home.
Like the stars, Soul won't turn under the sky.

Mind and Soul have crowded
The plate of earth, like ants.
Secretly, a curtain is opened
To the ones looking for a crack there.

Now the rose sapling is free from the thorn,
Because it is sure of the Heart.
It doesn't have any enemies;
There is no one to gather the rose now.

Be silent, be silent, O Heart.
Become an eye like the language
Of the iris and narcissus.
Keep looking at the garden.

159.

*L*ast night, the Heart like a drunk
Had fallen here and there
Because of Him.
The Soul acquired hundreds of languages
Like the iris
Because of His stature,
Which resembles a rose sapling.

Hearts are like sugar,
Full of sweetness because of His lips.
But once He is hidden,
They start crying like Ferhad. [288]

This body, which is made of soil,
Becomes hundreds of heaven's gardens
Because of His favor.
The wind coming from His side
Enlivens death, makes Jesus jealous.

He shows a caliph, suddenly, from nature,
Which resembles the stoke hole of a bath.
Baghdad starts praising Him
Because of the head of the devouts.

The angels in the sky find
The pleasure of their rosaries
Because of the light of His face.
The eyes of guidance,
The light of showing the way,
Were given to the worshipers because of Him.

Thousands of Souls are around Him.
He is at the center like a moon.
Going by, swaying like a drunk.
God saves Him from evil eyes.

The brightness of the full moon
Comes from the glory of His face.
The smell and color of ambergris
Of the hair of Shimshad,[289]
Coming down on his forehead,
Are curls that are also from Him.

What would happen if the world were destroyed
Because of the soldier of Love's Sultan?
The Soul of Souls would create
Hundreds of worlds again.

Even those looks in the eyes
Which torture lovers, favor kindness to beauty,
Those charms still come from Him.

You stepped on the sky with coyness, greatness.
In one moment the earth should understand
That the Sultan of Beauty was born
From Him
And grew with His kindness.

Hundreds of idols and idolmakers
Have fallen into commotion
Because of His beauty.
In the end, idolmakers start yelling
And quit idolmaking.

What is that? What kind of sun is that,
Shining at the sky of Beauty?
Why did this Fountain of Life
Overflow and become a sea?

Someone put his head
On the cover of Shemseddin's saddle blanket
At the temple where He is served.
But who could that be?
Shemseddin is such a man
That even the Archangel Gabriel
Would spread his wings under His feet.

Because of Him, Tebriz may open its secret,
The Eyes of the Soul start seeing,
And the eyes of the ones who are jealous
Become totally blind.

159.[290]

O Lover, Lovers, the time for Union has come.
A voice is heard from the sky, saying,
"O moon-faced ones, be ready."

O drunks, drunks, joy and pleasure
Come by holding His skirt.
He has held our chains.
We grabbed His skirt.

Fiery, strong red wine has come.
O grief, go to the corner and sit there.
O Soul who is thinking of death, go away.
O One who offers the wine, Cupbearer, come.

O my Beautiful!
Seven layers of sky are drunk
Because of You.
We are a crystal ball in Your hands.
Our being comes from Your Being,
Saying hundreds of thousands of times,
"Welcome," to this whole Being.

O sweet-breathed player,
Ring the bell every moment.
O drinking One,
Put the saddle on the horse.
Blow on our Soul,
O morning breeze.

O flute, the stories you tell us at night
Are so lovely.
Your Soul has the sweetness of sugar.
The smell of loyalty comes from your sounds
Day and night.

O beautiful-faced sun,
Start once more.
Play the same tunes.
Be coy with all the beautiful ones.

Be silent. Don't tear the curtain.
Drink from the glass
From which the silent ones drink.
Cover the others' faults.
Get into the habit of God.

160.

I told the Beloved yesterday,
"O, peerless Beauty,
Even the moon has become jealous of you
And is folded in two in the sky."

You were beautiful.
Now your beauty has increased a hundred fold.
You were the doorkeeper.
Now you've become a Sultan.
You resembled Joseph.
Now you've acquired the glow of Mustafâ [291]
And His manner.

O Fairy, let me praise you tonight,
Because tomorrow
You cannot be described by words.
While describing you,
Tomorrow, earth and sky
Will disappear altogether.

Let me take the opportunity tonight.
I will be your servant, your slave.
Tomorrow the angel will pass out of himself.
The Arsh[292] will be torn.

Suddenly, a storm breaks out,
Leaving no door, no roof.
How could a fly be able to fly?
Not even an elephant could withstand it.

Suddenly, His beauty, His light
Shines inside of this storm.
Every particle smiles with joy,
With the light of the morning sun.

Those poor particles regain their beauty
And their charm
From that one whose face is like the sun
And become attractive particles again.

161.

I am at the head of the table
Of His favor and loyalty every night.
I am the guest of the Sultan every night.
I am the guest of the One
Whose kingdom would be eternal.

One night, a monkey sat at the lion's table.
Don't insist, be fair.
Where is the monkey?
Where is the lion?

Even the heart of the brave
Is scared by the sword of the Sultan,
Of bleeding drop by drop.
What insolence is this?
In God's name, this is not right,
It is not right.

It's alright if a lion cub
Claws its mother's face.
But if you aren't your own enemy,
Don't even try to play with Him.

The one who drinks milk from the lion
Becomes a lion.
He isn't human anymore.
I have seen so many human-shaped creatures.
They were really monsters.

Noah was in the shape of a human,
But he was the flood who wiped out humans.
If there is a fire in one particle,
It must be the light in there.

I am a sword. I shed blood.
I am soft and, at the same time, hard and sharp.
I resemble this temporary world,
Pretty outside, troubles inside.
I am Absence in reality.

162.[293]

Verse 3589

O wayward, amiable friend,
The one who became insane!
His cup had fallen from the roof,
His secret became known.
Here, look. Once he was sent
To the lunatic asylum.

He was looking for water
By turning around the pool like a thirsty One.
Suddenly he fell into Our pool
And, like dry mint,
Got wet and became relish for our bread.

O learned man, don't take these words seriously,
Close your ears, don't hear this spell.
He became a legend with our spell.
What has happened to him
Has become a story for everyone.

People won't forget this.
Ears won't get free of this earring,
Because He took thoughts
And intelligence from heads
And poured them into a cup
Like grain ready to become ground in the mill.

O Soul, don't take this too lightly.
Don't think it is just play.
Try to work with your Soul,
Take a personal interest in that.
So many combs turned upside down
Because of His black curly hair.

Don't be over-confident with your mind.
So many masters in this world
Stand upright, wail
And cry more than the pole of Hannane.[294]

I've been separated from Soul.
I tore my clothes like a rose.
I became such a shape
That even my mind became a stranger to me.

That drop of mind
Has been annihilated in His sea.
That particle of Soul has been spent and depleted
On the way to the Beloved.

I should be silent,
What's the use of this candle
In front of the One whose light
Makes the sun and moon like a moth?
I should extinguish this candle.

163.

This Love puts a tray on top of His head
And walks around from street to street, yelling,
"Wherever there is death, I will give life,"
Adding, "No cheating, no deceit."

He continues, "I become a meal with My favors,
My kindness goes around,
But never comes to an end.
Where is the beggar who would
Come and fill his bag?

"I overwhelm you with pearls,
Sometimes with poison.
Recognize Me, know Me.
You are like a bushel in My hand.

"I will make gold mines
If a small grain comes and submits itself to Me.
If there is a steep, bare hill,
I'll make an endless sea of it.

"Poverty is from you, favor from Me.
You'll be satisfied; I'll give away a fortune.
I'll put out hundreds of satins for the silkworm,
Dress him with hundreds of heavy garments.

"I give such a crop to helpless ones
Who have never sown nor harvested;
I give such a feeling to the dervish
Who has neither suffered nor struggled.

"I'll pour a fountain of sweets
On the narrow heart of sugar cane.
I'll put nice, happy thoughts
In the mind.

"Ride your horse in the way of religion,
If your horse gets hurt, don't worry.
You'll find Yilki, [295] a wild, unbroken horse,
Instead of a pure one."

Be silent, don't say, "It is not like that."
Don't look for anything but God's favor.
The Halva [296] of contention
Is overflowing from the pot to the fire.

See every particle to know of a certainty
From the light of God's Shems of Tebriz.
Every particle starts talking
If there is pleasure in talking.

The end of

Bahr-i Recez

Footnotes:

1. "I don't like anything to set.": This refers to a story about Abraham's disappointment that the sun and moon, which at first he thought were God, always set and about his desire for a permanency in God. Koran VI, 76-79.

2. "You have created...": Refers to story of creation as described in the Koran, VII, 10; X, 3; XI, 7; XX, 59; XXXII, 3; L, 38; LII, 4.

3. "The beginning...": Koran, XXII, 1.

4. "Compassion of the universe": Koran, XXI, 107.

5. Dal: Eighth letter in the Arabic alphabet. A line descends slightly to the right, then curves left.

6. Elif: First letter in the Arabic alphabet. A straight vertical line.

7. Hodja: Slang for man.

8. Sheddad: Founder of the city of Irem who announced himself as God. Koran LXXXIX, 7.

9. Nemrud: Ruler of Keldenishtan in the time of Abraham who threw Abraham into the fire. God turned the fire into a rose garden. Koran XXI, 57-70.

10. "God does whatever He desires": Koran XIV, 27.

11. Ayse: The name of the hodja's lover.

12. Kible: Direction to Mecca for Muslim praying.

13. Remil: Arabic word meaning sound. Ancient way of fortune-telling based on sounds.

14. "Woe to every slanderer and defamer": Koran CIV, 1,2.

15. Parrot: Koran, XI, III, 49-110.

16. Ferhad & Shirin: Persian love story.

17. Leylâ & Mecnun: Arabic love story.

18. Karun: According to legend, an exceedingly rich man who hid his treasures.

19. Sheyyad: A musician, minstrel.

20. Reward of Love: Koran, L, 11-21.

21. Müstef'ilün: This represents the meter of this portion of the poetry of the Dîvân-i Kebîr.

22. Staff: The rod of Moses.

23. Rinds: Certain type of Sufi.

24. Mustafâ: The Prophet Mohammed.

25. Shuayb: Father-in-law of Moses.

26. Beyazid: Bistami, died in 874 A.D.

27. Kible: Direction Muslim faces when praying.

28. "God's compassion...": Koran XXI, 107.

29. "Two arrow throws...": Koran LIII, 9.

30. "Level of much closer": Koran LIII, 9.

31. Mescid-i Aksâ: The chapel of Jerusalem.

32. Houris: Beautiful women in heaven.

33. Hel-etâ: Mature man. Koran LXXVI, 1.

34. "God does whatever...": Koran III, XIV, 27.

35. Gazel 20: Recited at the wedding of Mevlana's son Veled.

36. Huma: Legendary bird which eats bone. The person on whom she casts her shadow becomes a Sultan. Also called stately bird.

37. Nesrin: A variety of rose.

38. Sema: Ritual of the Whirling Dervishes.

39. Halva: Sweetmeats.

40. Berbad: Musical instrument.

41. Hel-etâ: A mature man, mentioned in the Koran LXXVI, 1.

42. "God is the only one...": A saying called "Lâhavle" attributed to the Prophet Muhammad.

43. "You give Your kingdom...": Koran III, 26.

44. God does whatever...": Koran III, XIV, 27.

45. Lâhavle: Praise.

46. Helie: Medicinal herb called terminalia.

47. Hel-etâ: A mature man, mentioned in the Koran LXXVI, 1.

48. Oshur: A 10 percent tax owed to the government.

49. Nun & elif: Arabic letters.

50. Rabbena: A name of God.

51. Lebbeyk, Lebbeyk: "I accept Your invitation." As pilgrims turn around Mecca, they say these words.

52. "He doesn't need...": Samed. Name of God mentioned in the last chapter of the Koran and the second verse names of God which mean, "Everything, everybody needs Him, but He needs none."

53. Âsaf: Vizier of Solomon.

54. "Giant fairies...": Koran, XXXVIII, 31-33.

55. Çigil: A city in Central Asia.

56. Zünnâr: A rope girdle formerly worn by early Christians in Turkey.

57. Deccâl: A legendary one-eyed evil person who will come just before the world ends.

58. Vâmik & Azrâ: Persian love story written by Unsuri (d. 1040). Lovers like Romeo and Juliet.

59. Bâyazîd: Melometi Sufi who died in 875.

60. Senâî: Died in 1130.

61. Attâr: Died in 1221.

62. Arsh: Throne of God. Ninth level of sky.

63. Hel-etâ: Koran LXXVI, 1.

64. Abû-Alî, died 1037. Famous philosopher Ibn-sina.

65. Abu-l Alâ, died 1057. Famous poet Al-Maari.

66. "God does whatever...": Koran III, XIV, 27.

67. Abu-l Hasan: An Arabic philosopher.

68. Abu-l Alâ: An Arabic poet. Died 1057 (Ibn-i sina), 1037 (Abu-l Malri).

69. "Stay away...:": Hadis (Al-Dimna).

70. "Apples": The story of Joseph and Zeliha. Women cut their hands because they were peeling apples and trying to watch the beauty of Joseph at the same time. Koran XII, 30-31.

71. Hel-etâ: A mature man.

72. Ihvân-i Sefâ: Clean brothers, Sufis on the same road, a secret Moslem sect which applies pre-christian Greek philosophy to Moslem.

73. Hizir: Legendary person who attained immortality by drinking the water of life and comes to aid in a critical moment.

74. Kible: Direction Moslems face to pray.

75. "God's lion...": Signifies Khalife Ali.

76. "Melt & cast...": Koran XXXIV, 10-11.

77. Süha: A small star in Ursa Major.

78. Leylâ & Mecnun: Famous Arabic love story.

79. "Game...": Arabic saying.

80. "Time...": Arabic saying.

81. "Israelites...": Story from Koran.

82. "You will be...": Koran V, 24.

83. Hodja: Slang for man.

84. Galinos: Famous doctor who lived in the city of Bergama and who died in 131 A.D.

85. "Patience is the key...": Old saying.

86. Throne of God: Koran II, 255.

87. Min ledün: According to Sufis, a knowledge comes to the Heart without books or teacher. Based on Koran XVIII, 65.

88. Rinds: Certain Sufis. A jolly, humorous, unconventional man.

89. Kurban bayram: Moslem festival of sacrifice. Tenth day of Arabic month, Zilhicce.

90. Door of heaven: Ridvan.

91. Moor hen: Seagull.

92. Husrev: A Persian mythological hero.

93. Ferhad: Persian love story.

94. Mecnun: Arabic love story.

95. Vâmik: Love story.

96. Gazel 39: Written about the return of Shems from Damascus.

97. Saffron: Old saying. Saffron made people laugh.

98. Bedehsan: City famous for its rubies.

99. "His eyes...": Koran LIII, 17.

100. Nimrod: An impious king who is said to have cast Abraham into the flames.

101. Rüstem: A legendary man with great power.

102. Kevser: River of heaven.

103. Indian: Symbolizes night. The Turk symbolizes day or brightness.

104. Kadir: The night the Koran came to Muhammad.

105. Fairies: Old folk tale. The fairies lived around fountains and waterfalls.

106. Hurmuz: City in Central Persia.

107. Urbuz: The name of a Mongol ruler of this time.

108. Oguz: An old Turkish tribe.

109. Bulgar: A Turkish tribe.

110. "I make an oath...": Koran XC, 1.

111. Edhemoğul: Died in Damascus, 777-778. His life resembles Buddha's.

112. Kevser: The river of heaven.

113. Hakan: Head of the Khan.

114. Sencer: Ruler of Khorosan Selcuks from 1117 to 1157.

115. Kible: Direction that Moslems pray.

116. Elif: First line of Arabic alphabet. A straight line.

117. Cim: A letter from the Arabic alphabet. A curved line.

118. Cam: A wine glass.

119: Kible: Direction Moslems pray.

120. Muhre: Burnished glass ball used to polish paper.

121. Five and six: The five senses and six dimensions.

122. "Food rained...": Koran II, 57.

123. "Produce no harm": Khadis Al Cami al sağiyr II, p. 192.

124. Râfizî: The one who quit. Later Suni called him Shii.

125. Ömer: First with Suni.

126. Alî: Considered first by Shii.

127. Leylâ and Mecnun: Arabic love story.

128. Hârûn: Legendary rich man from Moses' tribe. Koran XXVIII, 76-82.

129. Cim; sad; elif; nun: Letters of the Arabic alphabet combined to resemble the face.

130. Mecnun: Arabic love story.

131. Cim: Curved letter in Arabic alphabet.

132. Hizir: Legendary figure who is a Godsend.

133. "His mole on your cheek": Refers to spots on the moon.

134. Cem: A mythological Persian king.

135. Yurt: Tent or country.

136. "I'll fill...": Mevlana put dirt to Kemal-i Kowval. Menakubi-Arifin T. Yazici. P. 94-86, I-942.

137. Kevser: River of heaven.

138. Sencer: Selcuk king (d. 1167).

139. Min ledün: According to Sufis, the knowledge which comes to the Heart without teachers or books. Based on Koran XVIII, 65.

140. Kaaba: Direction.

141. Elif: Letter of the arabic alphabet.

142. Husâmeddin Hasan: Died 10/25/1284. Precursor of Mesnevi. He followed the path of Mevlana with Sultan Veled after the death of Mevlana.

143. Verses 896-898 (gazel 71) do not appear in Gölpinarli's translation of *Dîvân-i Kebîr*. Most probably, this is due to misnumbering.

144. "From the Soul's sweetmeat...": Taalav. Koran III, 61-64, 167; IV, 61; V, 104; VI, 151; LXIII, 5).

145. Cem: Mythological Persian king.

146. Elest: "Am I not your God"? Koran VII, 171-173.

147. Bairam: Religious holiday.

148. Âsaf: The vizier of Solomon.

149. Isfahan: Mode of Near-Eastern music.

150. Kullah: A conical hat.

151. In Gölpinarli's translation of *Dîvân-i Kebîr*, there is no gazel 83. Most probably, this is due to misnumbering.

152. Hârût-Mârût: Two angels in the Koran who blamed the people for being bad. God told them it was because the people had lust. The angels couldn't understand, so God gave them lust and sent them to earth, to Babel. During the day they would teach magic, and at night they would get in trouble with women. One angel wanted a woman's favor, and in order get it, he taught her the names of God. When she went up to the sky, God punished her and made her the planet Venus. When asked what kind of punishment the angels on earth would get, God caused them to be hung upside down at the well in Babel. Magicians still go to the well hoping to learn tricks. Koran II, 102.

153. Tacik: Tribe in Central Asia.

154. "Where is the sky, where is the rope?": Old Persian proverb.

155. Batha: Another name of Medina.

156. Kafdagi: Fabulous mountain inhabited by Donjinns.

157. Kible: The direction for Moslem prayer.

158. Ahmed-i Muhtar: The Prophet Muhammad, Koran LXI, 6.

159. Hayder-i Kerrar: A hero who attacks like a lion, back and forth.

160. Isrâfîl: Angel who blows the trumpet on judgement day.

161. Leylek: Stork.

162. Vulture star: Name given a certain star in the west side of the sky.

163. Reveal: This order comes from God to the Prophet Muhammad many places in the Koran.

164. Houris: Beautiful women in heaven.

165. Hizir: A legendary Godsend who attained immortality by drinking from the water of life and comes to aid in a critical moment.

166. Isfahan: Name of a city in Persia.

167. Me'vâ: One of the eight paradises where martyrs and prophets are allowed to go.

168. Syriac: Northern Iraqi Christian.

169. Abû-Hurayra: Muhammad's disciple. Nicknamed "father of cats." He used to carry a leather bag. He said, "I received two bags full of knowledge from God's messenger: one for people; the other, I couldn't say. (d. 677).

170. Lâhavle: The beginning of the Koran states that only God makes it possible to change from one condition to another.

171. Verses 1180 & 1181 were included in Farsi in Gölpinarli's translation of *Dîvân-i Kebîr* as follows: 1180: Iy bes ki ez avaz-i dus vamendeem ez rah men/ ey bes ki ez avazi kos gum kerddem hargah men. 1181: Key varehani zin kosem/ Key varehani zin dusem ta deressem/ Der dovletet der man/ O hirmangah men.

172. Yemen: The country.

173. Sea of Adan: A gulf from whence the best pearls come.

174. Hasan: Common name.

175. Macun: A sweet fruit with medicinal value.

176. Ceyhun: A river in southeast Turkey.

177. Leylâ & Mecnun: Arabic love story.

178. Ca'fer-i Tayyâr: Flying Cafer, one of the uncles of Muhammad who lost his arms in war. The Prophet said he will have wings in heaven.

179. "Owner of this watering sky": Koran LI, 7.

180. "We have heard": Koran II, 285; III, 193; XXIV, 51.

181. Ferhad: Persian love story.

182. Mecnun & Leylâ: Arabic love story.

183. Four foundations: Fire, air, water and earth.

184. Jaw bending: Sign of contempt.

185. Tie the jaw: Moslems tie the jaw of a corpse.

186. "I created the skies because of You": Khadis-i Kutsi.

187. Mecnun & Leylâ: Arabic love story.

188. Uhud: Mountain near Medina.

189. The sky has been described in the Koran XIII, 2; XXXI, 10.

190. Pivot: According to Sufis, the universe is a body for humans. Humans are the soul of the universe. There is one Man among humans who is the soul of humanity. All the Universe turns around him. He is like a Pivot. That's why he is called (Kutup) Pivot. He turns around himself.

191. Hasan or Abu-l Hasan: Husâmeddin. Follower of Mevlana. Precursor of Mesnevi. Succeeded him. (d. 1284). Koran XXXVI, 26.

192. Yemen: The country.

193: Leylâ & Mecnun: Arabic love story.

194. "I accept Your invitation": Lebbeyk, Lebbeyk, or Pilgrim's yell.

195. Nev-rûz: New day when the sun enters the sign of Aries. The beginning of spring.

196. "And the last one went further": Ahadis-i Masnavi, p. 67-68.

197. "Truly we did open...": Koran XLVIII, 1.

198. "We stay in line": Koran XXXVII, 165.

199. Rüstem: Persian mythologic hero.

200. "We'll return to Him": Koran II, 156.

201. Forelock: Koran XCVI, 15-16.

202. Shahne: Police magistrate.

203. Ishmael: Son of Abraham.

204. Circis: A prophet who was killed by his people seventy times and came back to life seventy times.

205. Semurg: The fabled King of the Birds.

206. Sünbüle: The sign of Virgo.

207. "...my tribe knew...": Koran, XXXVI, 26.

208. Müstef'ilün: This represents the meter of this portion of the poetry of the Dîvân-i Kebîr.

209. Vessel: We created man, and we know what doubt his self gives to him, and we are closer to him than his carotid artery. Koran, 50-16.

210. "Going under the basin": To extinguish the candle.

211. Abu-l Alâ & Abu-l Hasan: Abu-l Alâ was an Arabic poet. Abu-l Hasan was an Arabic philosopher.

212. Huten: Chinese beauty.

213. Mustafâ: The Prophet Muhammad.

214. "...become apparent": David asked, "My God, why did you create man?" God said, "I was a hidden treasure. I wanted to be known. I created man." Badî-al Zaman Firûzan-fer, Ahadis-i Masnavi, 29.

215. Dal: the 8th Arabic letter of the alphabet. The beginning of prayer.

216. Oxen of body: Sign of Taurus.

217. Hyacinth-like eyebrows: Sign of Virgo.

218. Rüstem: A legendary man with great power.

219. Mecnun & Leylâ: Arabic love story.

220. Hu: Beginning of a Dervish chant.

221. "Four overflowing rivers": Before his ascension, the Archangel Gabriel showed four rivers to the Prophet Muhammad. Two of them were the Euphrates and Tigris. The other two were the rivers in heaven.

222. "...should soil his beard": Not a complete translation. This verse in Farsi is: Iy kun-i har kez hasidi isi buved tesvis-i u Sed Kiri har der kun-i u sed suz-i sek der ris-i u.

223. "More deviate than animals": Koran VII, 179.

224. The elephant of Soul: According to folklore, when the elephant sees India (its own country), it becomes exuberant.

225. Kadir: The night of Kadir. The night the Koran is revealed to the Prophet.

226. Pole of Hannane: Crying pole. Prophet Muhammad leaned on it while giving his sermon. It was a branch of a date tree. Later they built a pulpit in the mosque and, according to legend, a crying noise came from that pole. The crying stopped when the Prophet put his hand on the pulpit.

227. Ruh: Name of legendary bird like the phoenix, able to catch an elephant. One of the chess characters is named for it.

228. Ibrahim Edhem: d. 777-778 in Damascus. Like Buddha, this son of a king gave up everything for the way of Truth.

229. Abû-Bakr: Flying from Mehhe, the Prophet stayed in a cave with him on the way to Mechna.

230. The 7th & 10th verses of this gazel were recited during a Sema. (Eflâkî-T. Yozici, 20-a)

231. "We dressed in paper clothes": In these days, someone with a grievance who wanted to get the attention of the ruler would dress in paper clothes and put a candle on top. (Gölpinarli)

232. Rum: People from the land of Rome. (Asia Minor, denotes day, light.)

233. Zenci: Denotes black, night, darkness.

234. Hizîr: A legendary Godsend who attained immortality by drinking from the water of life and comes to help in a critical moment.

235. Hizir: See footnote #234.

236. Hamel: Sign of the zodiac.

237. Sünbüle: Sign of the zodiac. Virgo.

238. Hakan: Oriental potentate.

239. Mansür: Hallaj Mansur: Famous Mystic who was killed in 922 because of his beliefs.

240. Heten: A generous man who lit campfires at night for those who had lost their way.

241. Abû-Bakr: Flying from Mehhe, the Prophet stayed in a cave with him on the way to Mechna.

242. Hakan: Oriental potentate.

243. Leylâ & Mecnun: Arabic love story.

244. "Come": Taalav: Koran III, 61-64; IV, 61; V, 104; VI, 151; LXIII, 5.

245. Kharezms: Rulers in Central Asia in 12th & 13th centuries.

246. Keyhusrev: Persian king (d. 519) who took Babel in 554, freed the jews and united Persia with Mesopotamia. Persian name is Kurus-i Kebir.

247. Tablets of God's decree: Levh-i Mahfûz.

248 Müstef'ilün, Müstef'ilün: This represents the meter of this portion of the poetry of the Dîvân-i Kebîr.

249. The numbering "Verse 1712" appears twice in Gölpinarli's translation of *Dîvân-i Kebîr*, as the last verse of gazel 132 and again as the first verse of gazel 133, most probably due to misnumbering.

250. Verse 1756 does not appear in Gölpinarli's translation of *Dîvân-i Kebîr*, most probably due to misnumbering.

251. Hasbek: Someone close to the palace.

252. Taylasan: Material which turns around a turban and then connects with the hands and waist.

253. Âzer: This name is mentioned in Koran VI, 74. May be uncle of the Prophet Abraham.

254. Halva: Sweetmeats.

255. "God has brought": Koran II, 3.

256. "On the glass of the bath": It was an old custom that the glass on public baths had drawings. Sa'di (d. 1293) mentioned that someone saw satan in his dream as a handsome young man, and he said to the devil, "Why do they draw your ugly picture on the glass of the bath?" The devil answered, "What can I do? The pen is in the hand of others."

257. "Really, we will return...": Koran II, 156.

258. Zün-nûn: Letter of arabic alphabet.

259. Lâ: No, absent.

260: Illâ: There is nothing but Him.

261. Mescid-i Aksâ: Holy shrine in Jerusalem.

262. "God is calling": Koran II, 221; X, 25.

263. Shuayb: The father-in-law of Moses.

264. Medrese: Moslem theological school.

265. Travel: Koran III, 137; VI; XVI, 36-20; XXV, 42.

266. Remil: Sand. Denotes old fortune telling with sand.

267. Birds of Abraham: Abraham asked God how He brought death to life. God said, "Go get four birds. Tear them to pieces and put them on top of the mountain. Now call them." And four birds came flying. Koran II, 260.

268. Tambur: Stringed instrument.

269. Ya Hu: Names of God.

270. Six-doored chapel: Earth. The five senses and six dimensions.

271. Ca'fer-i Tayyâr: Flying Cafer, one of the uncles of Muhammad who lost his arms in war. The Prophet said he will have wings in heaven.

272. Houris: Beautiful women in heaven.

273. Leylâ & Mecnun: Arabic love story.

274. Karun: Legendary rich man. Moses' cousin.

275. Seyh Zün-nûn: Melameti Sufi (d. 859).

276. Düldül: White horse of the Prophet.

277. Lover's grass: A kind of grass which fades quickly.

278. Âzer: This name is mentioned in Koran VI, 74. May be uncle of the Prophet Abraham.

279. Leylâ & Mecnun: Arabic love story.

280. Kible: Direction Muslims face to pray.

281. Ursa Minor: Star of Ul-ker.

282. Houris: Beautiful women in heaven.

283. Abû-Alî, died 1037. Famous philosopher Ibn-sina.

284. Abu-l Alâ, died 1057. Famous poet Al-Maari.

285. Cabbar: Bully.

286. Kamer's Moon: Sign of zodiac. Cancer.

287. "Source of malice...": Koran XII, 53. Nefsi emmare.

288. Ferhad & Shirin: Persian love story.

289. Shimshad: Gracefully grown young person.

290. The following gazels were translated by Gölpinarli at a later date than the rest of this meter, *Bahr-i Recez.* The numbering is his. The numbering for gazel 159 appears twice, first as beginning with verse 2079, and second, as beginning with verse 3567.

291. Mustafâ: Prophet Muhammad.

292. Arsh: Ninth heaven. Throne of God.

293. Gazel 162: According to Eflâkî, this gazel was told to one of the Katib-al-esrdr (The Secretary of Secrets). Eflâkî said that Fahreddin Sivasi (45b-46 1259) changed some words while copying Mevlana's words and became insane.)

294. Pole of Hannane: Crying pillar (pole) while the Prophet Muhammad was preaching.

295. Yilke: Wild, unbroken horse.

296. Halva: Sweetmeat.

Designed by
Archibald Valentine Associates
Los Angeles, CA

Typeset in Caslon 224 Book & Duc de Berry by
Powerhouse Publishing
Los Angeles, CA

Printed & Bound by
Publishers Press
Salt Lake City, UT